Modern Poetry in Translation
Series Three, Number 10

The Big Green Issue

Edited by David and Helen Constantine

MODERN POETRY IN TRANSLATION

Modern Poetry in Translation
Series Three, No. 10
© Modern Poetry in Translation 2008 and contributors
ISBN 978-0-9559064-0-4

Printed and bound in Great Britain by Short Run Press, Exeter

Editors: David and Helen Constantine
Reviews Editor: Josephine Balmer
Administrators: Deborah de Kock and Angela Holton

Submissions should be sent in hard copy, with return postage, to David and Helen Constantine, *Modern Poetry in Translation*, The Queen's College, Oxford, OX1 4AW. Unless agreed in advance, submissions by email will not be accepted. Only very exceptionally will we consider work that has already been published elsewhere. Translators are themselves responsible for obtaining any necessary permissions. Since we do sometimes authorize further publication on one or two very reputable websites of work that has appeared in *MPT*, the permissions should cover that possibility.

Founding Editors: Ted Hughes and Daniel Weissbort

Subscription Rates: (including postage)

	UK	Overseas
Single Issue	£11	£13 / US$ 26
One year subscription (2 issues, surface mail)	£22	£26 / US$ 52
Two year subscription (4 issues, surface mail)	£40	£48 / US$ 96

To subscribe please use the subscription form at the back of the magazine. Discounts available.

To pay by credit card please visit www.mptmagazine.com

Modern Poetry in Translation is represented in the UK by Central Books, 99 Wallis Road, London, E9 5LN

For orders: tel +44 (0) 845 458 9911 Fax +44 (0) 845 458 9912 or visit www.mptmagazine.com

Modern Poetry in Translation Limited. A Company Limited by Guarantee. Registered in England and Wales, Number 5881603.
UK Registered Charity Number 1118223.

- 109 Pedro Serrano, 'Swallows', translated by Anna Crowe
- 111 Mangalesh Dabral, two poems, translated by Sudeep Sen
- 114 **Naomi Jaffa**, Aldeburgh 2008
- 116 **Yi Sha**, five poems, translated by Simon Patton and Tao Naikan
- 122 **Antjie Krog**, 'the unhomely'
- 126 **Farzaneh Khojandi**, two poems, translated by Jo Shapcott
- 130 **Rose Scooler**, 'Mica Parade', translated by Sibyl Ruth
- 136 **Tomas Venclova**, three poems, translated by Ellen Hinsey
- 142 Peace, Poety and Palestine
- 144 **Franz Hodjak**, six poems, translated by Peter Oram
- 150 **Zsuzsa Beney**, five poems, translated by George Szirtes
- 154 **Cesare Pavese**, three poems, translated by David Douglas
- 159 **Eugeniusz Tkaczyszyn-Dycki**, five poems, translated by Bill Johnston
- 163 **Jerzy Harasymowicz**, four poems, translated by Maria Rewakowicz, with illustrations by Swava Harasymowicz
- 169 **Eugene Dubnov**, two poems, translated, with the author, by Vernon Scannell, Anne Ridler and John Heath-Stubbs

Reviews

- 172 **Cecilia Rossi** on translations of Pura López-Colomé, Dulce María Loynaz and Mercedes Roffé
- 177 **Paschalis Nikolaou** on Richard Burns's *The Blue Butterfly*
- 181 **Belinda Cooke** on Sasha Dugdale's Elena Shvarts
- 185 **David Constantine** on *Poems from Guantánamo* and two Hafan Books
- 188 **Josephine Balmer**, Further Reviews

- 192 Notes on Contributors
- 199 Two back issues
- 203 Subscription form

Contents

1	Editorial
5	The next issue of *MPT*
6	**Bewketu Seyoum,** poems, translated by the author and Chris Beckett
14	**Martti Hynynen,** five poems, translated by Mike Horwood
18	**Oliver Reynolds,** 'Rosenegg's Night'
20	**Waldo Williams,** 'Spring 1946', translated by Jason Walford Davies
23	**Pascale Petit,** four poems
30	**Rocco Scotellaro,** poems, translated by Allen Prowle
45	**Robert Saxton,** sonnets from Hesiod's *Calendar*
54	**Anna Lewis,** 'The Wash-house', from the *Mabinogion*
60	**João de Jesus Paes Loureiro,** two poems, translated by Stefan Tobler
63	**Antônio Moura,** three poems, translated by Stefan Tobler
67	**Mary-Ann Constantine,** 'Notre Dame de Port Blanc', from the Breton 'Itron Varia ar Porz-Gwenn'
78	**Terry Gifford,** Ted Hughes, Translation and Ecopoetics
82	**Pauline Stainer,** six poems
88	**Jeff Nosbaum,** 'Cape Weavers'
90	**Siriol Troup,** three poems
93	**Dante,** *Purgatory,* Canto xix, 1-36, translated by Mark Leech
96	**Wulf Kirsten,** 'village', translated by Dennis Tomlinson
98	**Wulf Kirsten,** 'Bleak Place', translated by Stefan Tobler
102	**Elisha Porat,** three poems, translated by Cindy Eisner
104	**Anne Cluysenaar,** two poems
107	**Anna Crowe,** 'The Mysterious Starling'

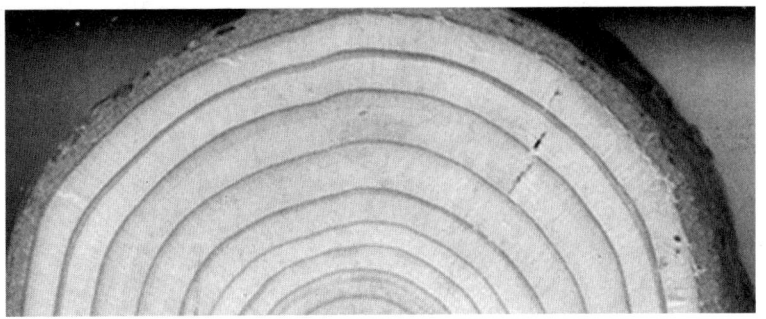

Editorial

Genesis 1:28 is a bad start, for sure. That and the demonization of women – first Lilith, then Eve: altogether a very bad beginning. Dominion over the earth and misogyny, it is no accident that at the outset they get coupled up. Hard to recover from a start like that. Millennia trying to grow out of it, and still not clear. Of course we can't just blame our religions – Rome was emptying Africa of its beasts, for the Circus, even without a Holy Book as premise – but among the uncivilized, among the primitive, there have been attitudes towards Mother Earth which, to put it mildly, would have done less damage. But Civilization arrived on their shores, pushed into their forests, spread over their plains, rose over their mountains, with weaponry, diseases and a quite peculiarly murderous cast of mind.

The harm we do the planet increases with our ability to do it. You can get a long way in the destruction of forests with fire and the axe, and our ancestors did. But thoroughly to poison the rivers and the seas and to clutter up space with toxic debris, only Progress can manage that. Know-how, cleverness, the inventions that are, in Oppenheimer's phrase, 'technically sweet'. He said, 'When you see something that is technically sweet, you go ahead and do it and argue about what to do about it only after you've had your technical success. That is the way it was with the atomic bomb.' Perhaps we need some primitive taboos, things we would never do? For the planet, once thought to be big, turns out to be small. So 'Trash, and move on!' won't answer any more. There's nowhere to go. This is it, earth, our dominion. (Though bet your life there's an elite somewhere, the real avant-garde, the Elect, the Righteous, even now preparing a Starship Free Enterprise, to lift off for pastures new, bide there a while, trash them, move on.)

Editing *MPT*, we never know what to expect. We may think we do, but come the contributions, come the surprises. That was certainly the case with 'Palestine'. And some of the surprises are in the gaps: what we expected and didn't get (hence, in 'Palestine', our Instead of an Editorial, to fill a gap). Striking in the postbag this time were the number of pieces, understood by their authors as 'green', which had to do not with saving any of our fellow creatures – cod, tiger, aquatic warbler – but with the unkindness of humankind towards its own immediate kith and kin. So a good deal in this 'Big Green Issue' treats injustice, the unfair distribution and use of land, hateful oppression. Peter Kropotkin, anarchist, revolutionist and natural scientist, appalled by the application of the Darwinian law of the survival of the fittest to human affairs, to the socio-economics of our living together, searched the animal kingdom for instances of survival by 'mutual aid'. That was his way of answering back. He knew that without mutual aid we, as a race, cannot prosper. A century later we know that without mutual aid we will die. We will cause a mass extinction and be extinguished in it.

The harm we do one another is inextricably connected with the harm we do to the rest of the living planet. In the frequent wars of the Ancient Greeks there was a convention – doubtless not always observed – that you would not poison your enemy's wells nor grub up his olive trees. The olive became a symbol of peace precisely because it needs many years growing in peace before it will crop. And without clean water we die. Consider then the policy – for it was a policy – to exterminate the Native Americans by exterminating the buffalo on which their lives depended. General Sheridan, asked should he not urge the white hunters to go easy (they killed three and a half million buffalo between 1872 and 1874), replied, 'Let them kill, skin and sell until the buffalo is exterminated, as it is the only way to bring lasting peace and allow civilization to advance.' The Native Americans (who killed c.150,000 in the same two years) used almost all of the buffalo. The whites only wanted the skins. They left the rest lying, along with the Indian ponies which they also made a point of slaughtering. Civilization, pushing West, was very good news for the vultures.

There is a passage, which at times has seemed very easy, from idly or deliberately wiping out another species to wiping out our brothers and sisters in humankind. Think of other humans as animals and do to them what you usually do to animals. The British arrivals in Tasmania hunted the natives to death. They organized hunting parties, wore the jackets, blew the horns, and hunted the Tasmanians into extinction. All that remains of the Ancient Prussians, exterminated in a crusade by the Most Christian Order of the Teutonic Knights, is place-names. And who knows what lore and languages were erased with their peoples in Amazonia? So, here, a poem about Buchenwald is 'green' in the sense that it shows what humans will do to other humans – in a place overlooking the humanist heartland of Germany, where there was a beech forest. The Camps, Oradour, villages in Vietnam and Palestine, battlefields and mass graves world wide, these are indelible marks we have made on the lovely face of the earth.

It is both encouraging and chastening to see how well the earth does when we, having done our worst, get out of the way. Involuntary parks spring up. There was a nice one along the Berlin Wall, on the western side at least. There's another still in the demilitarized zone between North and South Korea. Best of all though is Chernobyl. Such biodiversity now on the poisoned land! Earth recovers, Earth does better without us. From Nature's point of view, we don't matter. In time – infinitely spacious time – Earth will even recover from our final deed, another mass extinction, and homo sapiens, evolution's unhappy error, will have been one little incident in a very brief passage.

Only from our own point of view do we, as a species, matter.

Nothing else cares whether we live or die. And really that ought to encourage us to participate in survival rather than in extinction. In one form or another life on earth will go on. Whether we are part of it or not, is up to us. Our famous technology will help – but only if our consciousness (awareness and conscience) changes first. We have to change our minds.

The earth is beautiful, wonderfully complex and beautiful in its interdependencies, its myriad ways of living together. For many centuries (a heartbeat in geological time) the arts have been a medium of its admiration. Nothing else we know of in the universe is equipped to love, admire and cherish the earth as humans can. We can love, pity, cherish, admire in a way that no other creature as yet thrown up by evolution can. So if we die out, if we exterminate ourselves, earth will survive, recover and continue *lovelessly* – a huge deficit, which itself will go unfelt. It's a strange thought, an earth going on without love – unloved, and with no memory whatsoever of all the good and wise and beautiful things we did and all the love we felt.

David and Helen Constantine
August 2008

The Next Issue of MPT

The next issue of *Modern Poetry in Translation* (Third Series, Number 11, spring 2009) will be called 'Frontiers'.

Every issue of *MPT* crosses frontiers. Contributions come in from all over the world. Copies go out world-wide. And whatever their subjects, the translations themselves, out of many languages, cross frontiers of space and time. In *MPT* 3/11 we want to concentrate on that essential act, and make an anthology of many kinds of going-between and crossing-over. There are frontiers between species, countries, creeds, classes and generations; between the sexes, between life and death, between then and now . . . And poetry has always gone out to these boundaries, to survey them and to cross them. Some passages are customary and welcome; others are more like smuggling and transgression. Some borders are open; others are walled, barb-wired and mined. We invite submissions – principally translations, but versions, after-images, reflections and original poems also, that will encounter and cross as many frontiers as possible.

Submissions should be sent by 1 February 2009, please, in hard copy, with return postage, to The Editors, *Modern Poetry in Translation*, The Queen's College, Oxford, OX1 4AW. Unless agreed in advance, submissions by email will not be accepted. Only very exceptionally will we consider work that has already been published elsewhere. Translators are themselves responsible for obtaining any necessary permissions. Since we do sometimes authorize further publication on one or two very reputable websites of work that has appeared in *MPT*, the permissions should cover that possibility.

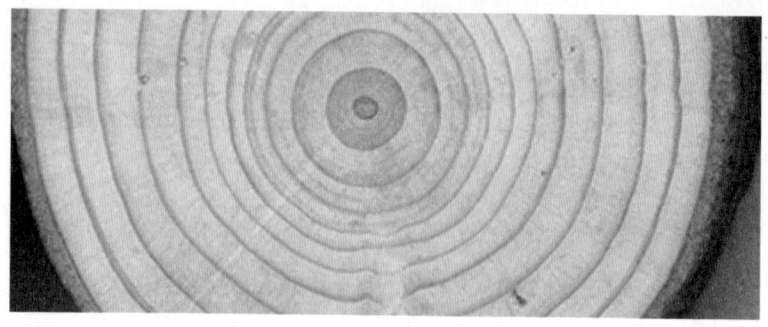

Bewketu Seyoum
Poems
Translated by the author and Chris Beckett

Bewketu Seyoum is a popular young Ethiopian poet and writer from Mankusa in Gojjam, north-west of Addis Ababa. He graduated from Addis Ababa University with a degree in psychology and English. His first book of Amharic poems, *Nwari Alba Gojowoch* (*Unmanned houses*) was published in 2001 and has since been reprinted three times. He then published a book of short stories, *Berari Kiteloch* (*Winged dreams*), which he has read on the radio to great acclaim. Earlier this year, his first novel appeared, entitled *Inkilfina Idme* (*Sleep and Age*), and a second collection of poems, *Ye Sat Dar Hasaboch* (*Fireside Meditation*).

Brought up by a father who teaches English and a mother from a devout and literate family, Bewketu never found much resistance towards realising his dream to be a writer. 'My father used to present me with books and lots of opportunities to read and that has helped me. On my mother's side the priests used to tell me stories and narrate them in a unique dimension.'

Bewketu's poetry is highly regarded for being original in style, quick, witty and epigrammatic. He draws on the ancient Ethiopian tradition of *qene,* short religious poems with word-plays and multiple layers of meaning (so-called wax and gold), but also on the topical couplets still sung by minstrels in drinking houses around the country.

He lives in Addis Ababa with his wife.

In search of fat

Thousands of thin people, all skin and bone:
'Where is our fat?' they shout,
rummaging through valleys and trenches,
searching and searching, over hills, in the sky.
At last they find it, piled up on one man's belly!

So playful!

So playful,
the mountains run off
and rocks disappear,
our rivers are snatched.
Who are we? we ask,
but they do not know.
We give them their names
and they take ours away.
So playful,
the land can't be trusted
to be where it was,
whatever was centre
is borderline now.
So playful,
the farmers keep tilling,
clouds teem with rain,
but seeds are unable
to stand their own ground.

The surface of life

Even if we mix it
with a smile,
colour it with laughter or a joke;
even if we mix it all together
and pour it on the sea of grief;
the sea is so deep
that its colour will not change.

Peace

When our hands bend iron for sickles,
the heart starts to imagine
our enemies' heads as grasses.

A flower growing on a rubbish tip

The flower said:
'Why am I growing on the rubbish?
What is the use of sweetening nectar
or beautifying a petal?'

So I replied:
'I don't give a damn for the bee,
but a fly works hard
to find sweetness in this filthy world.'

Hunger in the desert

When I was starving in the desert,
I saw a camel chewing the cud.
I was so tired and my stomach begged for food!
So I opened the Book and started reading.
Even the animal chews, I read, *so why not you?*
Why don't you eat the chewing animal?
But on the other hand, the Book cautioned,
is the animal's hoof cloven?
I watched the camel chewing.
Its hoof was invisible, covered in sand.
But even if the hoof is hidden, even if the hoof
is invisible to me, I know it is cloven.

Asking forgiveness

Oh Lord!
We have no food or water.
We have no wisdom.
Please give us a heart
as big as our stomach.
Make it a size which fits
into our stomach.

The road to nowhere

The one who looks to be in a hurry.
The one who looks to be quick.
The one who drives a good car.
The one who wears designer shoes
and the one who goes barefoot.
All these intellectuals and illiterates
travelling up and down the road,
overcrowding it from top to bottom.
Look how they go back and forth
and never get to their destination!

The end of the world

The sins of Adam's children
fill up the earth's belly.
She becomes swollen like a balloon.
So we expect her to explode
but she fools us
that she is still alive,
while she melts down slowly in our hands
like a bowl of ice.

Elegy

The fall of every leaf diminishes me,
so when I hear a rustle
I send my eyes out of the window
to look at the trees in the yard.
Alas! where there were woods,
now I see flag-poles standing.
Men have swept nature's nest away
to build their cities.
The melody of the nightingale
has lost its immortality
and I am sitting on a dead land,
writing my elegy in the sand.

Shelter

Chased by the mother of fires, the sun,
men, animals and birds take refuge
in the shade of a tree.
But where should the tree go for shelter?

Untitled

In the beginning
the trees created us in their own image
capable of infinite life
capable of infinite deaths.
Then
the trees grew invincible
to show us that they are gods.

Meditation on the garden

Bunch of grasses,
untrimmed,
you appeared out of my yard
suddenly
and illuminated my spirit,
leading it to hope.

Bunch of grasses,
untrimmed,
you showed me
that the colour of hope is green.

Bunch of grasses,
you appeared suddenly,
as if you had descended with the dew,
you baptised me.

Then I said: 'He who was clad in flesh
and came into the world
but passed in vain,
failing to appease my pain,
He has come back,
clad in grasses,
and hurled away my burden!'

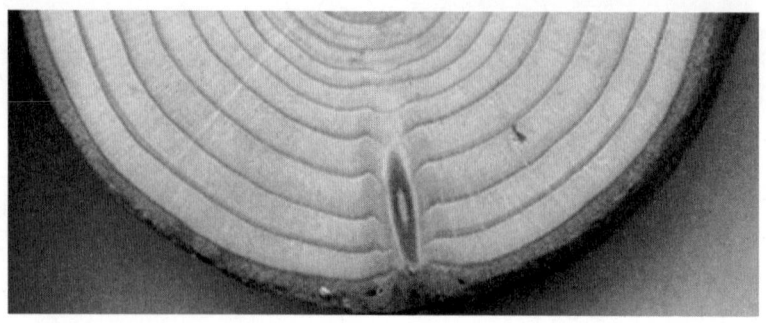

Martti Hynynen
Five poems
Translated by Mike Horwood

Martti Hynynen was born in Rovaniemi, Finland, close to the Arctic Circle in 1952 and grew up on the banks of Finland's greatest river, Kemijoki. His first collection, *saari, nimetön luoto* (*island, nameless rock*), was published in 1991 by Werner Söderström and his second is nearing completion. The five poems here are all from the first collection. The simple processes of nature, such as the sprouting of potato shoots, feature frequently in Hynynen's poems. Man's relationship to those processes, however, is ambivalent; sometimes in harmony, sometimes discovering identity (or effecting escape) through the natural processes of change and transformation and sometimes appearing to be in conflict with nature. All of these themes are present in the five poems here. Nature is portrayed as a source of wisdom and sustenance, and humanity as a species is able to attain that wisdom but also prone to impose its own interpretations on nature and sometimes to find itself badly mistaken. Despite this sometimes rather dark tone, though, the emphasis is on surviving, which Hynynen sees as a guiding principle of nature. The complete collection will be published in English translation by Cinnamon Press in March 2009 under the title *island, nameless rock*.

A Humble Observation

at the interment
of those thirty potatoes

there should have been
a majestic bird

crossing the heavens
forging its way north

which could later
have been interpreted

as a lucky omen

Profane Days

you put questions to me
so we walk back to the garden

settle ourselves down like seeds in an apple
that a hand reaches towards, then hesitates

Migration

at the very first stirring
my airtight, upright

sarcophagus breaks
into pieces,

each fragment
starting to turn green

even as it falls
and the seeds

sink into clay
coming up as small trees

and clumps of grass
ready to take root

in the cracks between
the town square's paving

Revelation

The stone will be rolled away from the earth cellar's entrance
and we'll fall to the ground

hands reaching towards the sky
each in our own way
even though we lack
the natural wisdom of the sacred

potato shoots

Mistakes

It was not spring
    with newly-grown grass
or fluffy moss creeping
    up the hanged man's leg to the fir tree,

it was the green glass of a smashed bottle
    along the top of the wall round the garden
to which the gate or secret door
    could not be found

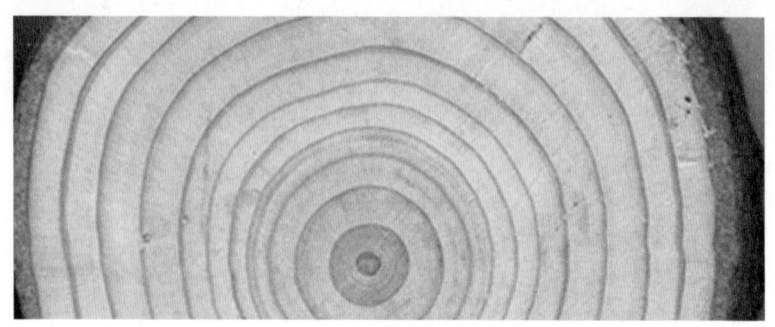

Oliver Reynolds
'Rosenegg's Night'
After Hermann von Gilm zu Rosenegg's 'Die Nacht'

Rosenegg's Night

As though stalking a hare
down meadows of mown hay
night steals closer with day
     unaware

Blue and green start to yield
to fallows hedged with shade
then sheaves and stubble fade
     with the field

Day grown suddenly old
sea unsilvers the waves
names remembered by graves
    lose their gold

Blossom ghosts from a tree
the heart has one beat left
and night one final theft
    you   from me

Die Nacht

Aus dem Walde tritt die Nacht,
Aus den Bäumen schleicht sie leise,
Schaut sich um in weitem Kreise,
Nun gib acht.

Alle Lichter dieser Welt,
Alle Blumen, alle Farben
Löscht sie aus und stiehlt die Garben
Weg vom Feld.

Alles nimmt sie, was nur hold,
Nimmt das Silber weg des Stroms,
Nimmt vom Kupferdach des Doms
Weg das Gold.

Ausgeplündert steht der Strauch,
Rücke näher, Seel an Seele;
O die Nacht, mir bangt, sie stehle
Dich mir auch.

Hermann von Gilm zu Rosenegg (1812–64)

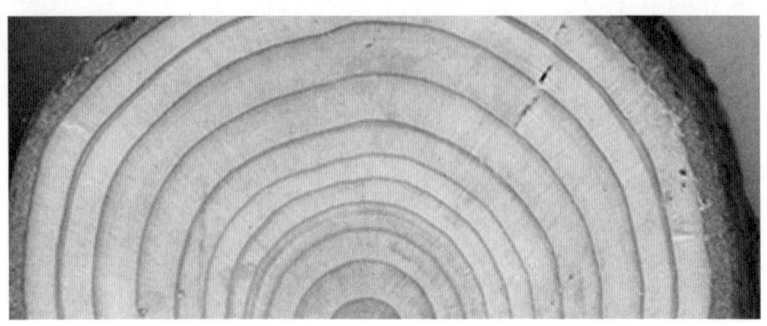

Waldo Williams
'Spring 1946'
Translated by Jason Walford Davies

Waldo Williams (1904–71) is regarded as one of the finest Welsh-language poets of the twentieth century. Translation assumes a particular valency in his case, since Williams is very much a liminal writer, one who lived his life in his native Pembrokeshire *across* the Landsker, that cultural line of demarcation between the Welsh-speaking north and the Anglicized south. Welsh was in fact Williams's second language.

'Gwanwyn' (1946), written during the first spring after the Second World War, is the only one of Waldo Williams's major poems that has hitherto not appeared in translation. One reason why translators have been unwilling to tackle the poem is the fact that it is among the most difficult of Williams's works. The complex and highly compressed syntax – 'telegrammatic', as one critic has aptly put it – presents the translator with a distinct challenge, namely to tease out possible meanings and to engage confidently with, and respond sensitively to, a range of subtle linguistic and imagistic combinations.

Added to this are the challenges posed by the poem's agitated half rhymes, its distressingly internalized, and often surreal, imagery, and its use of literary allusion. It was important also to try to communicate in translation the troubled intensity of the original's use of long, rhythmic lines in order fully to appreciate the power of the climactic — and, for Williams, uncharacteristically maledictory — ending. The horror lies in the fact that this new peace, and a new spring, serve only to mask man's instinctive inhumanity to man.

Spring 1946

'The turtle and the crane and the swallow observe the time of their coming; but my people know not the judgement of the Lord'
(Jeremiah 8:7)

Out of the elm's carbuncled bark, the span of its green in flight.
Out of the torn, compacted earth, the seam of its bright shoots.
Don't be fooled by your silver tongues, your smug waiting for tomorrow.
Out of your pounding of fellow-flesh, tapeworms burrow into brain and marrow.

All winter long your hunt was bold — a crazed new hunt on the last hunt's heels.
The spring's oppressive silence; in every yard a starved wolf's howl;
In the heart's dark chambers snarling she-wolves on heat,
In the wood men run to from the terror camps, the wood where the enemy waits.

Centuries of cities sacked to shore up the dreg-sodden fen:
Mothers, children, babies; people in pieces, for truth to go marching on.
Spring heats the boggy filth; above the lads' tracks a thicker vapour.
'Sign up. See the world.' The distant fen lurks. It will pull them under.

Look! in through the eyes of the sleepless swallow, life with no let-up floods.
In the shallow depths of spring beasts' eyes, the prancing of endless fields.
You of the fathomless eyes, darting through light into your brothers' essence,
May an eyeless god whip you in herds through the desert of your sad innocence.

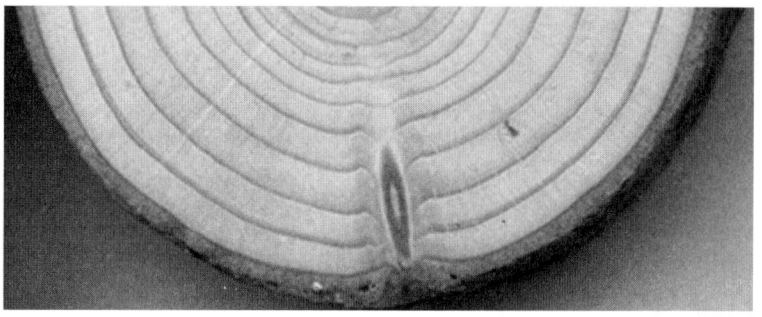

Pascale Petit
Four poems

Du Fu (712–70) is considered by many Chinese to be their greatest poet. My translation of his poem 'Ballad of the Old Cypress' is indebted to David Hawkes' *A Little Primer of Tu Fu* where the author provides transliterations and prose translations of thirty-five of Du Fu's poems taken from the anthology *Three Hundred Tang Poems*. I wanted to convey the visionary grandeur of the original, how the cypress becomes a cosmic tree. My poem is halfway between a fairly faithful free verse translation (as far as I can tell since I don't speak Mandarin and the original is in intricately formal Tang Dynasty Chinese) and a version; my main aim was to capture the expansive spirit of the poem. Du Fu wrote this while staying at the entrance of the Yangtze Three Gorges for two years, homesick for his thatched hut in Chengdu. The tree in Kongming's temple was considered dead but had suddenly started to resprout.

Like this translation, which grew from my travels in China, my poems 'Machapuchere (Fishtail Mountain)' and 'Creation of the Himalayas' arose from travels in Nepal. On a trek in the Annapurnas I only got as far as Remember Lodge because that day a landslide destroyed the bridge over Modi River and obliterated the trail ahead. I climbed through monsoon, then just before nightfall the sun came out and this sacred and unclimbable finned peak was suddenly revealed. The next morning I got up before dawn to view the whole mountain, and interviewed a local shaman before returning. On the flight back from Pokhara to Kathmandu the sky was clear and offered a panorama of the Himalayas, which looked pristine but are threatened by global warming and pollution. The poem 'Creation of the Himalayas' views them through Remedios Varo's painting 'Embroidering Earth's Mantle'. The spirit of the painter Georges Braque hovers behind 'Portrait of a Coast Redwood Forest with Mandolin', which is one in a sequence of poems from my stay among the giant coast redwoods of northern California.

To an Ancient Cypress
after Du Fu

You stand in front of Kongming's shrine
with branches of green bronze, roots of rock.
Your hoary, rain-soaked bark spans forty metres,
your black crown pierces heaven.
The shrine is long forgotten
but you still draw worshippers who come to gaze as clouds
cling to you from the ghostly depths of Wu Gorge.
An icy moon rises over the snowy peaks perched on your
   fronds.
You are the road winding me back to my hut near Brocade
   River,
where ministers and warlords once sheltered in the same
   temple
and giant trees towered over the ancestral plain.
My derelict doors and windows reappear on your boughs.

Even dying, your snakelike trunk coils, encircling the earth,
while in your lonely heights force-ten gales howl.
Your power is supernatural – only the Change-Maker keeps
    you upright.
If a vast hall should collapse and need new rafters,
the ten thousand oxen yoked to drag you
would turn and marvel at their mountainous load.
No carpenter could improve you since you already stun the
    world
though you have not yet reached your full girth.
Nothing could stop them felling you but who could wield
    the axe?
While phoenixes roost in your aromatic leaves
your bitter heart is riddled with termites.
Abandoned peoples, however neglected you feel, don't
    despair –
the greatest timber is always last to be used.

Machapuchere (Fishtail Mountain)

Waking in the Remember Lodge, I throw a glacier-cloak over
    my nightie,
shock myself awake

to find Fishtail silhouetted against the night.
Machapuchere the unclimbable, ally of shamans

who hang spirit-traps over the rope bridge to protect their
    children's school
from hail and avalanche,

who, in times of trouble, sing a mountain-chant
in stone-bass and ice-vowels, smoke swirling from their
    mouths,

as now my breath rises in dawn-drafts, up into eagle air
to be washed by the stars.

I am always on the flagstones of that mule path,
waiting for the accentor robin's morning mantra

before mud thunders down the landslide.
I will always climb until it goes quiet

and I can no longer hear Modi River's roar,
just to watch lightning skein the gorge in flash-waterfalls.

Yesterday I trekked almost as far as Ghandruk through
    monsoon.
The trail was a broken cascade.

Just before sunset, a hole cleared in the clouds, unveiled
the double dagger peaks,

a hole jagged as Shiva's third eye, which he may open
to incinerate the world.

The flanks gradually whiten in a morning-glory blue
and the rising sun lights up the first fin, snow blowing from
    the tip

until it catches fire.
And as I stand still as an unclimbed mountain, hour after
    hour,

each gully and glacier in the Annapurna Sanctuary emerging
     from my memory,
  I see how the river leaps into the sky, returning to
     its source –

  a Milky Way boiling with whirlpools and rapids; spiral
     mirror
  that gets darker and slower the further down the valley it
     flows,

  past tea-houses, straggling stalls, to the highway that winds
     back towards Pokhara.

Creation of the Himalayas
after the painting Embroidering Earth's Mantle *by
Remedios Varo*

They say we are just embroiderers
but when we are working well, our tower turns
into burnished fire and the mantle flows
from our fingers, tumbling through the air
in loops of delight. There are always men
trapped in our weave. The sky calls their names
and they climb, trying to reach back
through the clouds to our blue fingers.
They glimpse us over the Tibetan Plateau,
our needles flashing like nimbus.
Each dancing thread and singing stitch

must be precisely placed in its matrix.
Here where there is no oxygen
and the cold stings like a furnace,
our eyes spin like constellations
as we sew tapestries on our stellar frames
and let them drop through the slits in the walls.
We who have no voice hear
the snow's musical swirl across matter,
sense through our fingertips
a face emerging from Khumbu Glacier.
We weigh nothing, and our cloth when it's new
weighs less than us before it sets in its stone cage.
We never tire, knowing that the folds
that form under great pressure spurt wings,
and Chomolungma grows higher each year, homesick.
We add temples around her base,
work harder, the earth pouring through our palms.

Portrait of a Coast Redwood Forest with Mandolin

When the first ray pierces my canvas
I breathe on its shaft, make solar music.
It's in these early hours of a painting's life
that my palette becomes a mandolin, its thumb-hole

a soundhole plucked by brushes. My eye
darts from foliage to fog. I try to paint
the deep notes of these ancients,
how the bass rises from their roots

and spirals round their rings
before bursting into saturated light.
There is lake-black and mud-brown
a loon-shape brings up from the river bed

like primordial clay; red dots to raise
from drums of resonating bark.
There are greys to draw down from the clouds
like masks for the tree-gods' faces,

lightning to cast over their crowns.
The way they stir just before a storm,
the crack that opens in the sky – my first view
of the thunder woods in their electric groves.

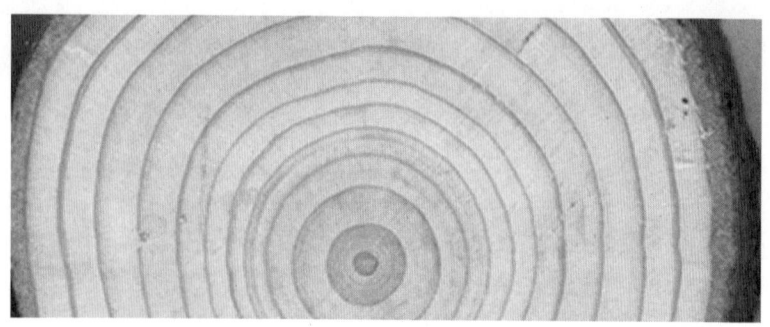

Rocco Scotellaro
Poems
Translated by Allen Prowle

Rocco Scotellaro never saw his poems published. In 1954, the year after his cruelly premature death from a heart attack at the age of thirty, *E Fatto Giorno* (*Day Break*), edited by his friend Carlo Levi, was published by Mondadori, and was awarded the Viareggio prize. He was the gifted son of a very poor family from Lucania, a mountainous and impoverished region of the Italian *mezzogiorno*. His parents made great sacrifices so that he could enrol at Rome University to study law, but the war and then the death of his father forced him to leave without completing his degree. He was of that young generation which saw the post-war years as a real opportunity to establish a just and egalitarian society, and to improve the material lives of the poor. At 23, he was elected as socialist mayor of his home town, Tricarico, and became actively engaged in the struggle for land reform. Inevitably, this brought him into conflict with the landowners, many of whom had welcomed his election believing that this son of a shoemaker could be easily manipulated. Victim of a political vendetta, he was imprisoned in Matera. The charges of corruption were spurious and he was acquitted after two months. He resigned as mayor and left for Portici, near Naples, where for some three years he studied at a research centre in agrarian economics. It was in Portici that he died.

One hears in these poems a voice, or rather, voices that had scarcely reached the ears of any public, let alone one given to reading poems. They narrate an archaic rural way of life dominated by the seasons, the harshness of place and weather, the need to feed one's family, but the sense of timelessness is sometimes disrupted by poems which relate contemporary events, such as the political defeat of 18 April 1948, the discovery that the agrarian reform plan had handed the peasants largely uncultivable strips of rocky ground, the death of his brother-in-law in the Greek expedition, the retreat of campaigning field-hands from the bosses' bully boys. Scotellaro, political activist that he was, is no populist poet. He lets us share his ambivalence towards a moment in history when the past and the possible future are in contention. He was never able to commit himself utterly to an intellectual environment where reform and political change were debated; emotional ties to an ancestral past, whose limitations and inertia so frustrated him, frequently brought him back from the city. The muleteer's daughter was ultimately more difficult to leave than the city girlfriend. His poetry is encamped in that border country where Raymond Williams also lived: pitched between attraction and repulsion, affection and irritation. The quarrel with others would have inspired, as Yeats claimed, a discourse of rhetoric, something Scotellaro no doubt kept for the hustings and public meetings. It was out of the quarrel with himself that he wrote many of the most telling poems in *E Fatto Giorno*.

The violets are children with bare feet

The leaves are fresh on the almond trees,
spring water rains from stone walls;
trotting lightly, the donkeys choose
the friendlier of the river's banks;
the girls with the darkest eyes
clamber on the squeaking cart, aloof.
March is a baby, laughing already, in its swaddling clothes.

And you can forget the winter,
who, bent by bundles of wood,
have told your beads,
mile after freezing mile,
to roast your face by the fire.

Now ticks come back to the horses,
in the stables flies stir the air,
and children with bare feet
charge upon clumps of violet.

Already you can smell the apples on the air

Already you can smell the apples on the air
and you can sleep the deepest sleep,
no moth flies in
to flutter round the lamp.
But I have never heard, in late October,
so many unfamiliar voices
reach me from the street;

my father was strapping up my trunk,
my sister repairing my clothes,
and I was having to leave to study
in a city which I did not know!
I felt my spirit turn to milk
when my friends spoke consoling words,
not moving, lonely and shy, from their doors.

Perhaps now I ought to leave in silence,
without a backward glance at anyone;
I'll seek some trade or other.
Here, a rag flutters on its threads,
and leaves from the apples scenting the air
are settling on my head.

Forlorn cuckoo, your call keeps us awake

All round the brown mountains
your colour has crept back,
our old September friend.
You've settled in among us.
When, fleeing the burnt stubble
of our fields, castaway crickets
screech at the doors,
our women have heard you quite close.
From the vaulted ceilings hang
strings of dried figs and green tomatoes;
there's a sack of hard wheat,
a heap of felled almonds.

Forlorn cuckoo,
your call
keeps us awake:
Yes, we'll trudge back along the paths
and, tomorrow, get down to work,
when water streams yellow again
under the furrows,
and the wind billows
our coats in the cupboards.

To the muleteer's daughter

I cannot live beside you any longer,
something stifles my voice.
You are the muleteer's daughter
and you take away my breath.
Because below us, in the stable,
the mules are restless, though asleep,
and your father, snoring nearby,
has not yet clambered on his cart
to beat away the stars with his whip.

The city girlfriend

Just as the sun, in early morning,
splinters behind the oaks,
so, love, as I look at you now, does my sight.
Your dress is flimsy as dawn's light,
lips like butchered meat,
breasts splayed apart.
I've been with you, and now I'm on my way.
Don't forget me,
or the field hands
snared in the headlights' sweep,
scattering into the fields like hares.

Capostorno

This gaunt and pieced-out land is cold
with the first bottle-green
now playing in my eyes.
With their oil-torches
they have set the mountainsides aflame
and, among mirrors of stone and fen,
they guide their mules.
By night they have trailed,
these starving owners of their plots.
They scan the whole plain,
but each has just a meagre strip.
They've reached this fecund land
to find the furrows numbered and marked.
On walking sticks
flutter their velvet coats,
flags of their destitution.

Torn trunks of oak
the flashing axe has turned
to scattered limestone bones.
Treeless, the place is empty
as a sky, or as a railing,
wide and gleaming, which just seems
a yellow flash of lightning.

Their very first tender bed of corn
at night was plundered by the shepherds
waiting just beyond the Acquanera ditch.
Far off, the cursing swells
with the fierce flood of the Bilioso,
making the wool of the flock shiver.
The marsh grass turns to water
the brains of sheep weary of winter.
Smitten by dizziness
they chase their tails,
banging their heads against rocks and trees,
like peasants losing sight of the horizon
when at last night falls.

Dead water ...... was churned up by the herd

He writhes among leaves of maize,
malaria bleeding and drinking him dry,
his skin like harrowed earth,
the gnarled hired man in his bed.
What mountains he has loaded on his back,
descending to the sea, braced by his crook.

Dead water in cursed mud holes
was churned up by the herd;
in the sun its litter yellowed.
He stares up at the loft,
beside him a pile of green wood;
hens scratch the ground
and the donkey's tail hangs
over the dung heap.
He has not seen the sunset bloom,
when the dogs moan
and a haze settles on the fold.

He had to turn back to the mountain,
go back to where he was born, so he could feel again
before he died, the pricking of maize on his skin.

Lent '48

The widow Quaremma was mad,
a dummy in an old apron,
spinning on her rope above the street
in the howling February wind,
target of the young terrors.
Expert stone throwers, they vented
the anger of their brooding fathers
for all the rains they waited for in vain
and for the meagre grain.
Covered by one of our coats
the heavens were even further from us,
and I would have liked to see
what part they were playing.
Behind the mountains' pen

the whinnying rollers on the Ionian
burst in our faces
and the sun thrust in our eyes
the flickering shadow of a candle.
Meanwhile, the sacred buds of earth
will not be closed.
Outside, the wind, pounding the doors,
may pipe the rebels' march,
but the blossoming almonds
picket the sown fields,
white horsemen of death.

The songs and the trap

Comes the snow and they set the trap,
then wait for the finch's chirp.
The schoolmistress reads to her young class
words of a love song for the songbird.
I loved both the songs and the trap.

Journey to the City

I have cast off my peasant slavery,
happiness no longer in filling up a glass,
freedom is what I have lost.
City of long exile,
of silence in a din of white noise,

where I must learn to tell my time
by the running of the tram,
and, unpacking locked bags,
timetable my tears, my smile.
How can I say goodbye to you, open arms of broom,
wide-shouldered woods
nudging the sky's blue face,
alliance of oaks and rocky steeps in the wind,
the flock gathered round the sleeping shepherd,
yellow earth that has cropped,
who are the woman who has given birth,
my brothers and the houses where they live,
the ways they take, like swallows, to return,
and the women and my mother,
how can I say goodbye to you?

I have lost my freedom:
at the hiring fair in July, so hot
that words could hardly carry,
I was bought by two dealers;
one handled the money, the other came to see me.
I have cast off my peasant slavery
of laden skies, of oaks,
of yellow earth that has cropped.
After a whole day
of the train's stops and starts,
at night the city appeared at last,
and it was not our moon,
and not the black table set at night,
and the mountains had got lost, somewhere along the way.

And together . . . we let out our curses

It is the time of year which drives us
to distraction all our own:
of rosemary white with dust,
of the whistling of swallows in the nest.
We are in the month before harvest:
the slightest shift of winds
and the men on the square turn nasty,
women leave their houses,
vendetta's leaders.
At the town hall they scream their want
of a crust of bread, a day's work,
and shoes, and roads, and everything.
And together, mayor and swallows and women,
we let out our curses,
which grow louder
than that of the housewife who has lost
her hen, and who tells everyone of her anger,
in the empty streets,
louder than that of the north wind
blowing low at the sun's flame,
raising the limp corn-stalks to our scythes.

Green is born

The sun's above lakes of mist
and now the hills are ships.
Green is born on the shining wild pear tree,
and even the rough scrub flowers,
branches in leaf on the mountain, grass on the shores.

To the fields I say how long gold oak has lived,
ringed by soft hornbeams
on the cowpath.
Listen, you can hear the panting of dogs,
the axe of the woodcutter,
when the earth feels the first warmth.

You have seen again the boys of their days
rolling their hoops of steel
in a race through thistles and flurries of dust.
You had some fun gently petting:
it was you who dashed the puppies on the stones,
snatched warm eggs from their nests,
crushed in your fist the bellies of sparrows;
squeezing the veins of velvet leaves
you bled Christ's initials.
You were the speechless lover
in a countryside so full of loves.
The goat, because the fruit is turning to ripeness,
looks round at you if you milk her,
but on the road which leads you far
from the gold oak
ringed by soft hornbeams
on the cowpath,
you will find the shed skin of the snake
in thorns which slavering cattle
have softened.

Matins

The procession began
already in the night.
I see the reapers in line
touching the star,
the only one to remain
at the tip of the twisting street.
In the long gut of my lane,
the iron-shod mules
ring out matins.

The full moon

Our beds fill with the full moon,
mules pass by on shoes of soft iron,
a dog gnaws its bone.
Under the stairs, you can hear the donkey,
its shudders and scratching.
Under the other stairs
my mother has slept for sixty years.

Lessons in economics

I asked you one day who planted
the sentinel spruce trees
I saw in the Dolomites.
I asked you many other things,
about the rock-rose, the myrtle,
sticky fleabane,
names not in my economics book.
One answer you gave, among others,
was that a father who loves his children
can only see them go away.

The shepherds of Calabria

To the sun-scorched houses by the sea at Paola,
through gnarled fig trees and along wide river beds
from which tumble dead rocks,
the Calabrians, down from the Sila,
sink their crooks into water,
not the cattle's trough any longer, but the sea.

The Royal Palace at Portici

What you first look at from beneath huge arches
is the sea, white below the black vault
of clouds released by the day.
Against the massive sweep of pines
a coral Naples blinks
its stage lights.
Of friends near and far
the memory falls, as the acorn falls
from the holm-oaks' swirl of cloud.

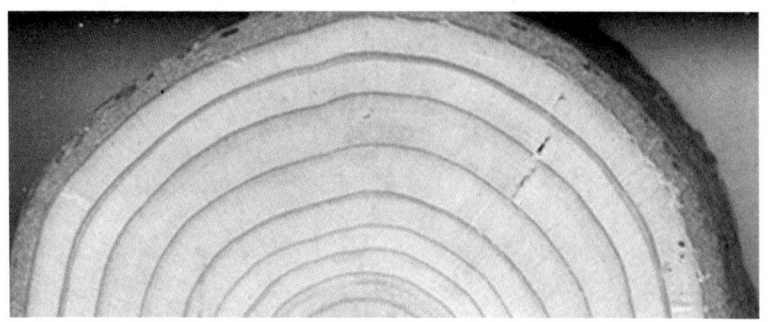

Robert Saxton
Sonnets from Hesiod's Calendar

Note
These two extracts are from a book, *Hesiod's Calendar* (not yet published), which attempts, in two sonnet sequences, to convert the heart of Hesiod's *Theogony* and the whole of the *Works and Days* into English poetry for the modern reader. I have no Greek, and have worked mainly from two translations of both poems into English: one in iambic pentameter by Dorothea Wender, first published as a Penguin Classic in 1973; and a literal prose version by Glenn W. Most in the Loeb Classical Library series (Harvard University Press, 2006). (More extensive use has been made of the Loeb than of the Penguin.)

My *Works and Days* (from whch all the following sonnets are taken) runs at 910 lines, compared with Hesiod's 828, the difference being accounted for by many passages I have amplified slightly to round off the meaning or elaborate an image, or to ensure that each sonnet is acceptably self-contained. My purpose was to render the whole poem in as lively and readable a fashion as I could, and in a coherent voice neither too grave nor too light (I was keen to avoid anything as blatantly detached as Byron's 'Hail Muse! et cetera', from *Don Juan*, while being unable to resist the occasional ironic anachronism).

Hesiod was a farmer-poet who lived in Boeotia, in mainland

Greece, around the beginning of the seventh century BC. A contemporary of Homer, his two best known works, the *Theogony* and *Works and Days*, are written in the metre of the *Iliad* and the *Odyssey*, the dactylic hexameter. *Works and Days*, addressed to a good-for-nothing brother named Perses, is full of worldly-wise grumbles and very practical and moral advice. It gives fascinating insights into the daily life of Ancient Greece, particularly work and survival in the countryside. In the first extract here Hesiod tells the story of the successive ages of mankind, from gold to iron.

VIII
And here's another tale you ought to know.
Once, divine and human beings were equal.
Under Cronos, gods made the men we call
the race of gold. Free of worry, sorrow

and old age, they lived on delicious wild food.
Death came to them like sleep. Every good thing
was theirs. Snake and scorpion bared no sting.
Each lived at ease, ruled only by his mood.

Happy, at peace, with every want supplied,
loved by the gods, they were blessed – but disappeared,
possibly in an earthquake or a flood.

In the wrinkled earth their spirits now reside.
Givers of wealth, and joy where music's heard,
they still have kingly rights. They are holy and good.

IX
Silver was the next race the gods made,
inferior to the gold – shorter, less clever.
To raise a child seemed to take forever:
for a hundred years the massive baby played

by its mother's side. Grown up, they lived brief,
anguished lives. Out of sheer stupidity
they couldn't stop doing each other injury;
and they forsook the gods, which brought them grief.

Their crime was lack of self-control, combined
with utter selfishness. Their chief disgrace
was neglect of sacrifice, leaving the altars bare.

Zeus, son of Cronos, was angry, and not inclined
to be lenient. He eliminated the whole race
for dishonouring the gods. Heathens, beware!

X
Then Zeus forged a third human race, from bronze,
worse than the silver dynasty – brutish, weird,
frightening. They loved violence and appeared
deaf to all but battle's shrieks and groans.

Fierce and strong, they ate no food from a farm,
only wild animals. No army could subdue
them. Their weapons were bronze, their houses too.
They killed each other in an orgy of self-harm.

Nameless, they ended up in the dark, chill
house of Hades, leaving behind no ghosts,
no tell-tale traces of themselves – not one.

Great soldiers though they'd been, Death with his will
of iron silenced their heaven-piercing boasts,
capturing from bronze the brightness of the Sun.

XI
And when this race was ushered underground,
the son of Cronos put another clan
upon this Earth, who immediately began
to prove themselves more just and good around

each other. This was the race before ours,
with human mothers – the so-called demi-gods.
Some fell in battle, powerless against tall odds;
some, seeking the flocks of Oedipus, by the towers

of seven-gated Thebes gave up the ghost;
while some for Helen's sake were killed at Troy.
Of many a brighter, posthumous story

's told, of landing off life's farthest coast
on the Isles of the Blessed: eternal joy!
This race of heroes well deserve their glory.

XII
Zeus made a fifth, iron race. I'm a member
of this clan – and wish I weren't, believe me.
By day we work and grieve ceaselessly,
by night some of us fade like an ember

cooling to ash in death. The great gods deal
a mixture of bad and good. Zeus will not spare
our kind. Babies will be born with grizzled hair.
Sons will defy their fathers, guests will steal

from hosts, true friendship will be all too rare.
Men will loathe parents who grow old too soon
and cruelly evict them from the family home.

They'll let whole towns fall into disrepair.
Wretched and godless, they'll worship the moon,
or nothing. Athens will sink with the rise of Rome.

XIII
Someone who keeps his word will be thought weak
and men will lavish praise unstintingly
upon the insolent and cruel, do injury
to better men, excel in double-speak

sworn upon oath with the sincerest eyes.
Envy will roam among the unenviable.
Fleeing Earth for Olympus to outwit the cull,
dressed all in white, so graceful and so wise,

will go the spirits Righteousness and Shame,
abandoning mankind to join the pantheon
of gods for their more virtuous company.

Honour burns with a bright yet faltering flame
we shield from winds unleashed where evil's done –
namely, on Earth, whose doom's our destiny.

*   *   *

XXI
O Perses, my brother, listen carefully.
Work till Hunger can only *wish* you dead
and till Demeter, revered and garlanded,
loves you (as I should) and fills your granary.

Though Hunger's loyal to him who fails to strive,
gods and good men have nothing but contempt
for those who choose to think themselves exempt
from work, like useless drones in a bee-hive.

Work brings the world's best things within our reach
and wins from the deathless gods a radiant smile.
It's far from shameful, if the truth be known:

quite the reverse. The lazy man's a leech,
bleeding himself – his blood's just bloodless bile.
Don't envy other's wealth: accrue your own.

XXII
Don't squeeze it from others, though: better, you'll find,
to receive it as a gift from the gods – a reward
for effort. If a man gets wealthy by sword
or stealth, as often happens when the mind

is clouded by greed and Shame gives way
to Shamelessness, the gods eclipse his sun,
his household shrivels, and he learns that no one
should expect ill-gotten gains to stay

the night. Moreover, he who harms a guest
or suppliant, or sleeps with his brother's wife,
or hurts an orphan child who can't yet speak,

or attacks his ageing father before he's dressed,
such a man angers Zeus. Before his life
has run its course, he'll be sorry he was weak.

XXIII
Now, open your heart to god-pleasing ways alone.
Do your sacrifices as the gods require,
with reverence and with heaven-seeking fire,
laying juicy thigh-bones on the altar-stone.

Let incense mingle with the evening's airs,
and with the dawn's when daylight's glimpsed again.
The gods will favour you, so other men
will never buy your land, though you'll buy theirs.

Don't feast your enemy, only your friend.
Be cordial towards your neighbour, who if trouble
comes to your farm is there at hand before

your kinsman's strapped on arms – you'll tend
to hang on to your cows. Pay back double
when you borrow: his loyalty's worth far more.

XXIV
Don't profit in disreputable ways,
for any gains such practices might yield
are just as bad as losses. A contract sealed
with an honest handshake and a gracious phrase

is how you'll prosper: don't betray a friend.
When someone visits, give if they give to you;
but if not, don't. This hoary maxim's true:
it's the giver who gets the best gifts in the end.

Giving's attractive, grabbing's quite obscene –
grim donor of death. Whoever gives ungrudgingly,
however much, takes pleasure from the deed

and feels his spirit grow. But he who's mean
enough to take even a small thing, shamelessly –
his heart freezes, turning brittle with greed.

XXV
Your household store is your foundation-stone.
It's good your wealth's at home, beneath your gaze.
Take what you need – that's fine. But a malaise
blights your spirit when you need more than you own.

Remember this: adding often to your store,
little by little, will one day make it huge.
Thus, brick by brick you'll build yourself a refuge
against Famine, fierce red-eyed carnivore.

It's best to take your fill when the storage jar
stands just opened or almost empty. Show
thrift in the middle: it's not worth saving dregs.

Pay your friend as promised, or you'll leave a scar;
with your brother, add a smile – have a witness, though.
Both trust and mistrust can hobble a man's legs.

XXVI
Don't be undone by a bottom-wiggling woman –
not if she's rootling in your granary.
This is one of a thousand shades of folly.
Be wise – for example, on the question of a son.

If you have two, you'll need more cash
and a longer life — yet two sons harm your health.
Just one on the father's farm increases wealth
and isn't such a drain. But don't be rash:

Zeus is ingenious at finding ways
to enrich a larger family. It's commonsense.
More hands, more work, more profit for your estate.

If profit's what you seek, this method pays.
Have many sons, and capitalize the expense
as a many-handed work machine. Procreate.

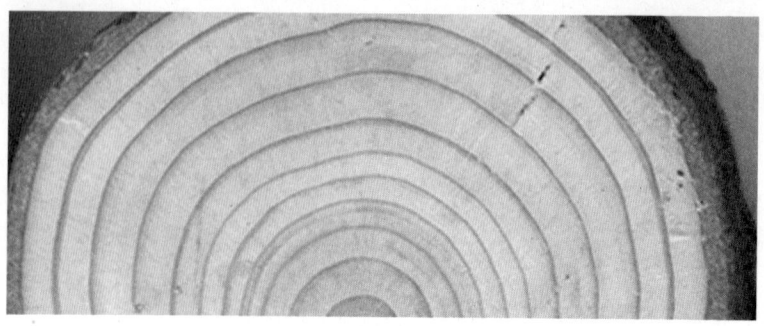

Anna Lewis
The Wash-house
Poems from the *Mabinogion*

Note
This sequence is drawn from the story of Blodeuedd, found in the *Mabinogion*, the major collection of Medieval Welsh tales. Blodeuedd is often thought to represent the natural world in human form; connections and tensions between humans and the natural environment run throughout the story. The sequence is told from the imagined perspective of Blodeuedd's maid.

Blodeuedd is created from wild flowers by magic, to be the bride for a young nobleman, but begins an affair with another man, who encourages her to kill her husband and appropriate his land. Their attempt at murder fails when her husband transforms into an eagle, and flies out of sight. Blodeuedd's husband is later reinstated by his uncle, a magician, who then pursues Blodeuedd, and turns her into an owl as punishment for her disloyalty.

The Wash-house

1
They knotted the roots and petals of wildflowers together,
waved their hands in some fashion or other,
and this droop of a girl sat up from the green.

A bride for the groom. She doesn't say much,
words stumbling out like young shoots.
'Don't remember,' she says,
so I show her where she used to be broom,
hitching herself from the dry soil under the cliff,
bees clamouring at each cup.

I show her where she was meadowsweet,
where she thickened the low field by the stream:
always thirsty, always twisting towards the white spurting
    water,
and insisting her roots in tough currents downwards,
wrangling the earth.

I show her where she was oak flower,
pouting in gangs between the spring twigs,
urging the green thud of water up through the trunk
and into the fizz of those thousand pink mouths.

'Next?' she says, wheeling hair round her finger,
but we are due back at the hall.
We stand for a few moments longer,
watch the fritter of blossom over the stream.

2
I help her tighten herself every morning,
tensing the hinge of each elbow, each knee.
She's all tendril, no sinew, apparently,
inclined to wilt,
unable to hold up her eyelids past dusk.

Bees clot at her armpits, and the back of her neck.
I swat them away, shake pollen grains
from her sheets. She complains
that everything I cook tastes like honey.

I try feeding her spoonfuls of salt,
give her garlic cloves whole.
I arrange candles in a throng round her pillow;
still, she tastes only sugar,
and sleeps from sunset until dawn.
Each morning, I scrape cold wax from the floor.

We stretch, bend, flex; she gets limper
as August shrinks to September,
and the first autumn fire blurts in the hall.

3
Autumn shakes into winter,
and we all settle down to our snow-pace:
slow hours under candle-light, patching and darning
the woollens, salting and curing small game.
I don't see so much of the girl –
her husband away, she keeps her door bolted,
won't meet my eye when we pass in the halls.

But we've had her pegged, in the wash-rooms and kitchens,
since the first snowdrop came shouldering up through the
    frost;
since the daffodils, all statuesque and deep blonde,
and the plum trees, scattering petals
over the still-rigid ground.

It gets no warmer,
sunlight shallow and brief on the field.
Her door bangs at midnight, and again before dawn;
she sleeps later, talks faster, flagrant
as the clematis limbering over her window.

4
She said nothing when she brought me her laundry,
the dress bloodied, stuck with wet feathers.
In the heat and fat steam of the wash-house
I powder the stains with salt-grains and soap-flakes,
suds billowing pink at my knuckles.

I imagine them both, hand-in-hand by the stream:
a low sway of cloud, a lingering dew on the grass.
She is jubilant, luminous as a pasture after strong rain.

I said nothing when she brought me her laundry,
her rose-hip lips twitching;
I scrub through the thickening steam,

see him lean down for a kiss, see her step aside
as the blade shivers clean from the bushes,
startling a red brace of wings from his chest.

5
But blood of his calibre can't be dismantled –
a limb, once pulled from these people, grows back.
He'll be gathered from the high branches
by well-practised hands,

and she will be blamed, with each crooked step
as he lurches towards his old shape,
his fingers flapping loose from the palm,
his spine pitching;
the drag of old wings, ghost-weight, at his shoulders.

He'll shake off the feathers,
grapple each hand to a fist.
The tilt of his spine unlocked and inclining,
he'll stamp a path home through the clover,
                                        the low blooms.

6
Odd evenings, I offer to fetch firewood from the copse.
On my way, I pinch scraps from the kitchen –
just cuts of fat, or green meat – slice them small,
and leave them under the nearest oak to the stream.

Sometimes she gobbles them down;
other times pecks with disdain, totters off.

She is much the same
as when she first arrived at the court:
unsure on her pins, pluck-plant-plucking
her way through the field; and quiet,
huge-eyed, with pupils that sway in the breeze.

Hard to say how she's changed:
not so gaudy, easy to lose in the darkening leaves,
as once she could dissolve into blossom,
and high meadow grass.

I never stay long; curtsey and turn back to the hall,
a bundle of dry twigs under each arm.

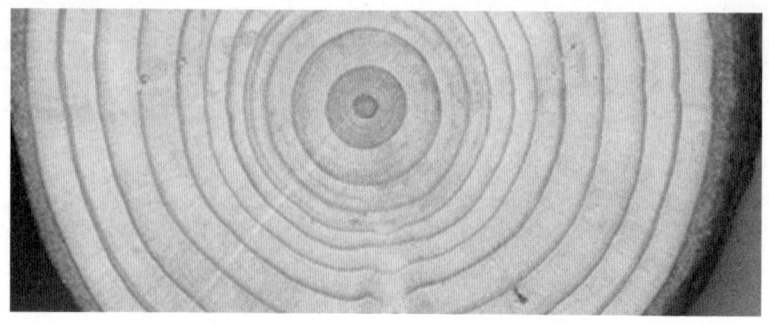

João de Jesus Paes Loureiro
Two poems
Translated by Stefan Tobler

João de Jesus Paes Loureiro was born in a small town in Pará, in the eastern Amazon region, and is a poet and professor of aesthetics, the history of art and Amazonian culture at the Federal University of Pará (UFPA). His first collection *Tarefa* was published in 1964, just before the military coup that brought a dictatorship to Brazil. *Tarefa* was confiscated and Paes Loureiro imprisoned for months. A prolific poet, his collections include the trilogy *Cantares Amazônicos* which has been translated into German and Italian. The focus moves from the Amazon's indigenous culture and history in the first book *Porantim* (1979), via increasing rural and cultural devastation in *Deslendário* (1981) to a large Amazonian city, *Belém*, and the many dispossessed who end up there, in *Altar em Chamas* (1982), the collection from which 'A Criminal Recipe' and 'Workers' are taken.

A Criminal Recipe

Let him be born.
The bed of poverty
               is a good measure . . .
He'll grow up without milk
and without greens.
The mud below the house's stilts
               is bound to give him
the tides' inheritance of worms.
It's a good thing he's got the samba groove.
He won't have schools
               nor a childhood.
And youth, would be better it didn't blossom
because the stem of his love
               has been castrated.

The day on which he goes out
               partner of the moon
(revolver in his belt
               and a decision in his eyes)
he'll be meat, peppered with bullets.

Workers

In the distance
                the neoclassical profile of churches.
Nearby
     the robust mango trees
and the sleepy gaze of green mangoes.
Oh: the sabiás and canaries
                        velveteen voices
perched, forever, on silent branches.

The factory whistle sounds
               – anxiety cloaked in smoke.
The workers, disposable pieces, stop the machines.
They sit on the edge of the pavement.
They open their aluminium containers.
They eat cold beans, the rice cold, the egg cold.
They have lost the pleasure of the sweet heat
of food giving itself to the loving stomach.
The knife and fork, the spoon are tools
with which, mechanically, they tighten, a screw, their hunger.
With the cogs of their mouths they chew.
Their jaws, bundled springs,
move in the oils of their saliva.

They are sat on the pavement
                      by the factory
and seem to be always in profile.

This being in profile
                  characteristic of things
we don't have the courage to look in the face.

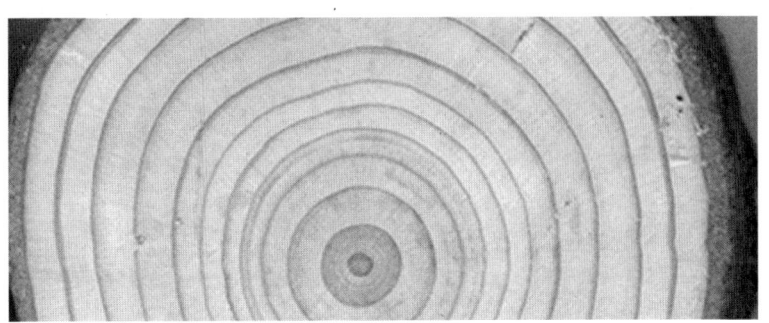

Antônio Moura
Three poems
Translated by Stefan Tobler

Antônio Moura was born in 1963 in Belém, capital of the state of Pará, in the Brazilian Amazon. Three collections of his poetry, and two of his translations, have been published: *Dez* (1996), *Hong Kong & outros poemas* (1999), *Rio Silêncio* (2004) and translations of Jean-Joseph Rabearivelo and of César Vallejo ('Considering coldly, impartially ...' starts with several lines from a César Vallejo poem of the same name).

Moura's poems have also appeared in many Brazilian journals and newspapers, such as *Cult* and *Sibila*, as well as in a number of contemporary anthologies in Brazil and abroad, including *Nothing the Sun Could Not Explain: 20 Contemporary Brazilian Poets* (2nd edition; 2003). He is currently being translated into Spanish, Catalan, German and English, and post-graduate book-design students are collaborating with Stefan Tobler on a possible exhibition of his poems.

Stains

A little black stain bird at the top of the day
The day that rises from the star's sleep.
Bird above the earth and whirr to nest
on the retinas of the man who, so small,
half-closes his eyes as he looks up.
A little stain on the earth
and a little stain in the sky,
reflecting each other in provisional images.
The stain that flutters and
the stain that crawls along,
but which also lifts itself when
the sight of the bird lends it wings.
Stain bound in the grass, observing
the black stain suspended in the blue,
both come from the world's secret womb
to the insecurity of nature's seen face.
Heavenly stain, earthly stain.
Between them just a murmur of wind
whispers dust and the cloud of existence.
Little black stains on the white of the day.
Bird and man, two dots, on the edge of silence:

Considering coldly, impartially . . .

Considering coldly, impartially
that man is sad, coughs and yet
settles in, and for, his reddened chest,
that he is nothing more than composed
of days, is a lugubrious mammal and combs himself,
considering this and remembering that day
is a fistful of powder from stars
that the night scoops and hurls
onto eyelashes before sleep,
that the sky has a violet sound over
this man's hair as he works in the setting sun
with the smell of gunpowder on his hands
and that this same man, when he enters
his lover, wants, perhaps, to return
That the sun is loneliness without the shadow of a doubt
That the moon is a conch in a magpie cloth
laughing into its craters over its fate
That the shadow that was born with me
waits for a movement from my body so that
she can, lovingly, repeat it
That the silence of a couple is love's voice
looking for a mouth to shelter in
and that those who don't understand each other
don't have words but leeches on their tongues
That, between its teeth, the wheel of fortune chews each
    failure
and that the devil sits smiling beside me drinking his shit
Remembering that tomorrow, tomorrow morning,
the sea could start to crumble my limbs of sand and
remind me that, at the same time,
I don't remember anything, except perhaps a womb

Omnisong

So wide that
to see itself
it has to turn
its own eyes into
mirrors: sky and sea
So without equal that
to have someone
to talk to, it has to
hear its own voice
spoken by all things

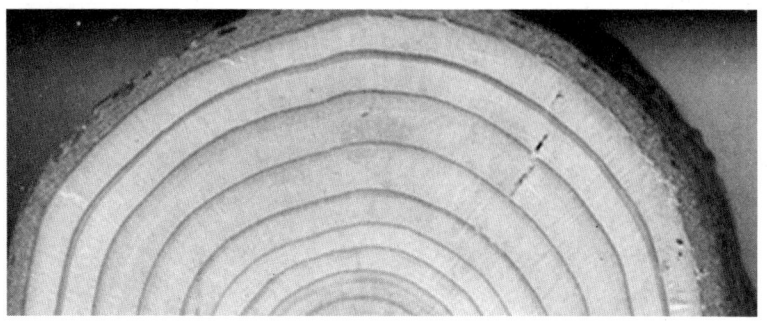

Mary-Ann Constantine
'Notre Dame de Port Blanc'
From the Breton 'Itron Varia ar Porz-Gwenn'

Fists, curled tightly like yours are now
Round fingers I give you one at a time.
But these are unfurling, these are green:
These are the bracken come back again.

The noise of the bombs on the rocky coast
Knocked small children over. We took to the woods
At night, watching the black sea flare.
Very few cameramen were there.

Jets ripped daytime black and blue
And the fishing boats burned. The air
Filled like a bruise with throbbing; the bell
Made the poor sea beat until

It reached the mother of our bleeding god.
They scanned and shot at us, and she heard:
Facing the grey boats under the sun
Each rock a fortress, each fern a man.

A million of them, a quick host sprung
From sand-dunes and ditches and quiet lanes.
They had no voices, rushing by,
Fear of Our Lady in their leafgreen eyes.

Beaches massed green. The dark grey boats
Fazed and blundering left the bay,
Scything the shoreline with panicky guns.
The soldiers were levelled but the war moved on.

We heaped up the fern-men in piles to die
Yellow and brown. The following year
Our coast was a moonscape, the sea stayed grey,
Crops rotted and the shoals and tourists kept away.

Slowly the land is forgiving us:
They come back singly. And I have brought you
Up here to watch the little fists because
Your dad was a soldier an hour or two.

Just as a metaphor is an idea anchored in a thing, so, in the Breton ballad tradition, a *gwerz* is a story anchored in a place. My poem was the unexpected by-product of my academic research – a response to a metaphoric moment in a remarkable place.

The place was Porz-Gwenn (Port-Blanc) on the north granite coast of Brittany, one afternoon in May or June. It was here, at the end of the nineteenth century, that the folklorist Anatole Le Braz happened upon an extremely rare ballad, telling the story of an English attack from the sea and the miraculous intervention of the Virgin. You can't help but believe it: the chapel built in her honour is still there, a tiny thing hugging the slope, with a huge roof that drops almost to ground level, as if wanting to protect as many people as possible. And, even more persuasively, the thousands of bracken-soldiers standing tall, fists clenched, facing the sea the whole length of the coast. The *gwerz,* sung by the seamstress Lise Bellec, is not a classic of the genre – it lacks dramatic structure – but its central image is overwhelmingly exact.

One or two elements in the poem perhaps need explaining. The literary metamorphosis of plant and human is ancient and widespread, but I had the middle Welsh text on the 'Battle of the Trees' particularly in mind. The soldiers are voiceless like the hapless living-dead fighters endlessly regenerated by the magic cauldron in the *Mabinogi's* story 'Branwen'. Like them, these fern men have been brusquely torn out of another world to come and fight our battles : I cannot think they came willingly. The poem is a lot darker than the *gwerz* from which it derives, but not without hope. The clenched fist, the curled baby-fist, is not always angry.

Anatole le Braz at Port Blanc, 1894. His account.

I had often heard my late mentor, M. Luzel, speak of the *gwerz* of Our Lady of Port-Blanc: it was said to be one of the oldest of our religious songs but he had never succeeded in collecting more than two lines of it – lines which neatly sum up the essence of the miracle that the song recorded.

> An Itron Varia ar Pors-Guenn
> A ra zoudardet gant radenn.

> Lady Mary of Port-Blanc
> makes soldiers out of bracken

'Do try and find out what comes before or after it while you are in the area,' he wrote to me in August 1892. 'It must be one of the more curious episodes from the period of our wars with Britain.' I did everything I could to please our honoured collector of folksongs; I knocked on every door, I accosted all the old folks reputed to be living vessels of oral tradition. Completely impossible to get anything out of them but those two lines. And then, last summer, as I was coming down the steps from the chapel, I heard someone singing in the sacristan's place. The voice rose clear and resonant through the open window into the calm evening air. I went in. Sitting cross-legged on the table was one of those travelling seamstresses who work from house to house. When she saw me she stopped singing.

'What were you singing there?' I asked her.

'Oh! nothing... an old religious song, nothing special. The tune is pretty though.'

I begged her to carry on, and then I got her to go through it again. She was singing the elusive ballad, the *gwerz* of Our Lady of Port-Blanc, so long sought for and always in vain. Here it is, just as she sang it, with all its gaps and inconsistencies:

1
Seiz lestr partijont assambles
Partijont a goste Londres,

Ma teujont war du Breiz-Izel
Wit massacri ar bobl fidel.

2
Ned Itron Varia ar Porz-Gwenn
E-man e zi war an dossenn,

E-man e zi war an dossenn,
A wel ar Zaozon deuz a belle

Itron Varia ar Porz-Gwenn
A ra zoudarded gant radenn,

A ra z,oudarded gant radenn,
D'ampich ar Zaozon da diskenn;

Kerkent, hi a deuz permitet
N'aje ar radenn da zoudarded.

3
Etre Porz-Gwenn ha Crec'h-Marted
A oa kant mil a zoudarded;

Ha pa zellent er e'hoste all
A welent mui pe gement all.

Tre Plouvouscant hac ar Porz-Gwenn
Holl a oant formet gant radenn,

Zoudarded vaillant, armet mad,
Prest da rei d'ar Zaozon combad.

Kement garrek a oa war drô
A oa n'am chanchet en forjô,

A oa n'em chanchet en forjô,
En forjô leun a ganonô.

Krec'h ar Gontess, war an huël,
Weler anezhan diabell . . .

Biscoaz sur ar Zaoz na welaz
Kement demeuz a bopulaz.

P'oant en dro d'ar vaz-pavillon
E clewent ar musik o sôn.

Tafêk, Perroz ha Louannek
A oa leun gouch a zoudarded.

Gentiles Rouzic ha Bono
Oa fortifiet trô war zrô,

Gant moguerio incomprenabl
D'ho spered ha d'ho daoulagad.

4
Tud Breiz-Izel, hed a coste,
A zo en spourôn nez ha de;

A zo en spourôn noz ha de
Gant aon na da goll ho buhe.

Mouez ar c'hanonô a groze
Ken a sklake tout ar c'hontre.

Gant an drouz demeuz an tennô
A goueze ar vugaligô.

Paour ha pinvik, iaouank ha coz,
A bartijont a greiz an noz,

Kwitâd ho zi hac ho mado
Ha decapi en forejô,

'N eur bedi ar Werc'hez Vari,
Jezuz he mab d'ho frezervi.

5
Ar Zaozon a lamp en Gweltraz
Prest da ziskenn an Douar-braz.

Imajô 'r Zent deuz bruzunet
Cloc'h ar chapel ho deuz loêret.

Laket deuz-han er wern-gestel
Da zôn wit ober an appel.

Kouet ê digant-hê er mûr dôn . . .
Eur veach bep seiz la e sôn,

Ewit ma lavaro tud Breiz
– 'Man cloc'h Sant Gweltraz er Ger-Eiz . . .

6
Pa 'c'h ê partiet ar Zaozon,
Oa rejouisset ho c'halon.

Pa int retornet d'ho c'hontre,
Deuz savet eun iliz newe,

Prenet eur gaer a gurunenn
Da Itron Varia ar Porz-Gwenn.

A plain version in English

1
Seven ships together they set off, they set off from near London,
And came to the coast of Brittany to slaughter the faithful people.

2
But our Lady of Port-Blanc has her house on the hill
She has her house on the hill and sees the English from afar.
Our Lady of Port-Blanc makes soldiers out of ferns,
Makes soldiers out of ferns to stop the English landing;
Instantly she granted that the bracken should turn to soldiers.

3
Between Porz-Gwenn and Crec'h Marted there were a
   hundred thousand soldiers;
And when they looked at the other side they saw more, or
   just as many.
Between Plougrescant and Porz-Gwenn, all were created from
   bracken:
Valiant soldiers, thoroughly armed ready to battle with the
   English.
Every rock in the area was turned into a fortress,
Was turned into a fortress, a fortress full of cannons.
Crec'h ar Gontess, up on the heights, can be seen from
   afar . . .
Never for sure had the English seen such a massive crowd;
As they stood around the main-mast they could hear the
   music playing.
Tafêk, Perroz and Louannek were stuffed full of soldiers,
The Seven Isles, Rouzic and Bono were fortified in every
   direction
By ramparts, astonishing to their minds and eyes.

4
The people of Brittany, along the coast, are in dread day and
   night
Are in dread day and night for fear they will lose their lives.
The voice of the cannons rumbled, so it shook the whole
   country.
The noise from the blasts made the little children fall down.
Poor and rich, young and old left in the middle of the night,
Left their houses and possessions and made for the woods,
Praying to the Virgin Mary and Jesus her Son to preserve
   them.

5
The English leapt onto the Isle of Gildas, ready to descend on the mainland.
They shattered the images of the saints and stole the bell from the chapel.
They hung it from the mainmast to ring out the call to arms
But it fell from them into the deep sea; once every seven years it rings.
And so the people of Brittany say St Gildas is ringing in Ker-Is.
When the English left, people's hearts rejoiced.
They went back to their lands and built a new church
And bought a most beautiful crown for Our Lady of Porz-Gwenn.

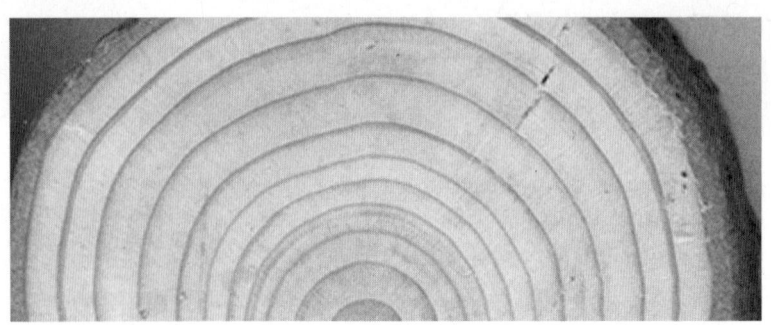

Terry Gifford
Ted Hughes, Translation and Ecopoetics

The co-founder, with Ted Hughes, of *Modern Poetry in Translation* in 1965, Daniel Weissbort, believes that the role of translation, as 'an integral part of [Hughes's] own oeuvre, just as the promotion of translation was perceived by him as part of his professional duty as a writer, seems largely to have been ignored' (2006: viii). Weissbort is currently writing a book on Hughes and translation, but has meanwhile edited *Ted Hughes: Selected Translations* (2006) which contains not only much unpublished material that spans his lifetime, but appendices giving samples of versions used by Hughes in his practice and a section headed 'Hughes on translation', that includes some early editorials from *MPT*.

Two features that might be thought mutually exclusive characterise Hughes' translations. The first is the way his translations were unmistakably 'Hughesian'. The second is expressed vividly by the Hungarian poet János Csokits who collaborated with Hughes on the work of Pilinszky and has written about their process in *Translating Poetry: The Double Labyrinth*, edited by Weissbort (1989). Hughes preferred to hear the poetic idiom of the Hungarian and the poet's personal style in Csokits' literal renderings into English, however odd and awkward this first text might seem. But Csokits recognised a special quality in Hughes's reworkings of his originals that he described as 'X-ray versions': 'It was almost as if he could X-ray the literals and see the original poem in ghostly detail like a radiologist viewing the bones, muscles, veins and nerves of a live human body [. . .] The effect is not that of a technical device; it has more to do with extra-sensory perception.' The paradox remains that despite his desire to remain close to the literal versions and retain a sense of their 'foreignness', his translations remained strongly Hughesian.

An insight into why this might be is offered by Neil Roberts in his chapter on Hughes as translator in *Ted Hughes: A Literary Life* (2006). Roberts points out that what Hughes chose to translate, and the manner of his doing so, continued preoccupations that were at the heart of all his work. Central to his whole literary project was an exploration of the connections between human inner nature and the dynamics of the outer natural world. Nowadays this might be called 'ecopoetry'. Roberts characterises it as 'a struggle to articulate spiritual experience in a vacuum of religious forms' and suggests that in his translations Hughes 'several times enhances the religious sentiment of the text'. One example from Hughes' *Tales from Ovid* (1997) indicates a clearly environmentalist agenda. In the Age of Brass, Ovid states, humans, although savage, were 'non scelerata tamen' (translated as 'but not yet impious' in the Loeb edition Hughes was using as an aid). In *Tales from Ovid* this Latin phrase becomes six lines beginning, 'But still/ Mankind listened deeply/ To the harmony of the whole creation'.

It is the failure of our species to 'listen deeply' to our environment in our interaction with it that has brought us to the current point of crisis in this relationship. In the growing awareness of this crisis 'ecopoetry' has come to displace 'nature poetry', the latter being thought of as complacent, escapist, sentimental and anthropocentric. Elsewhere I have discussed the reasons for this dismissal of nature poetry and the contradictions that such over-simplifications can produce (*Green Voices*, 1995, second edition 2009). Scott Bryson's *Ecopoetry: A Critical Introduction* (2002) offers three characteristics of ecopoetry:

'ecocentrism, a humble appreciation of wildness, and a scepticism toward hyperrationality'. Much traditional nature poetry would celebrate these qualities. But a cultural shift in our shared awareness of the current environmental crisis has produced a need for an ecopoetics appropriate to our times. It is to this awareness that Hughes' translation (and expansion) of Ovid speaks. A recent anthology of 'ecopoems', as declared by its subtitle, raises a number of questions about what an appropriate and successful ecopoetics for our times might be and what issues are raised by our evaluation of its products.

Neil Astley's anthology *Earth Shattering* (2007) includes some work in translation, from Neruda, Transtömer, Haugen and Tu Fu for example. (The latter's 'Dawn Landscape' is one of the most profound and moving poems in the book.) It also includes work by Ted Hughes, including 'October Dawn', written before the term 'ecopoetry' was in use, and 'If' which is about the self-destructiveness of our allowing water pollution. 'If' concludes, 'Already you are your ditch, and there you drink'. This poem is one of the weakest poems Hughes ever wrote because it is simply didactic propaganda. Seamus Heaney has said that poetry's gift for telling the truth lies in 'telling it slant'. Hughes admitted to me that when his poetry attempted to deal directly with environmental issues it did not seem to be 'the real thing'. Indeed, he warned against the temptation for poetry to become 'righteously embattled' with the enemy in what he called 'the Environmental Wars' (*Green Voices*, 174). 'October Dawn' can now be read as an 'ecopoem' in Astley's section headed 'Force of Nature' because it is 'telling it slant' as an ironic fantasy of the first signs of a new ice-age.

But Hughes desperately wanted us to sharpen our awareness of specific scientific evidence of our own self-destructiveness and he occasionally succumbed to the temptation to include the evidence in a poem. Also in *Earth Shattering* is his poem '1984 on "The Tarka Trail"' in which one line of poetry reads, 'Three hundredweight of 20-10-10 to the acre'. That's a line of poetry. The next one is 'a hundredweight and a half straight Nitram'.

Hughes wants the reader to feel the weight and know the data of what is being introduced into the environment, and especially the rivers, by a 'nature protector', birdwatcher farmer fertilising his fields. Hughes is aware of his poetic vulnerability to criticism here, but addresses the issue with the reader several lines later:

Now you are as loaded with the data
That cultivates his hopes, in this brief gamble
As this river is –
                as he is too

But although this poem may not be 'the real thing', don't we now need to know the data in our poetry? Don't we need to adjust our aesthetic in the urgency of our times to allow for the poetics to be informed by the data? So that, for example, 'cultivates his hopes' can have its full effect and so that the reader's feeling of being 'loaded' with facts can be transferred first to the river and then, by a specifically poetic device, to the farmer himself? We now know that Hughes was deeply read in the science of river pollution and was an activist on issues of water quality in the Southwest of England, even making a presentation to a public enquiry as part of a long campaign in the 1980s (Gifford, *Ted Hughes*, Routledge, 2008). And don't we need the explicit evidence that Hughes is both a passionate and knowledgeable ecopoet? When the Chinese ecocritic Lily Chen seeks to show her audience that Ted Hughes is an ecopoet concerned about water pollution, it is to the poem '1984 on "The Tarka Trail"' to which she turns (*Bestiality, Animality and Humanity*, 2005). But how good a poem is it?

It is clear that some influential poetry critics, especially in America, feel that the issues ecopoetry raises are not worth engagement. Helen Vendler and Marjorie Perloff, for example, have both not only ignored ecopoetry, but in Perloff's case been distinctly unscholarly in their treatment of the poetry of Ted Hughes (Roberts, 91). In the UK Edna Longley has made an interesting transformation from denying that Heaney might be regarded as a green poet, still less a post-pastoral poet, to championing Edward Thomas recently as 'a pioneering ecological poet'. But Longley's response to the critical reception of Hughes's *Birthday Letters* dared to ask the right question: 'Is Hughes's reputation being talked up in some way, and to hell with critical judgement, to hell with poetry?' (Longley 1998: 30) One is tempted to ask of Astley's anthology, 'Is ecopoetry being talked up in some way, and to hell with critical judgement, to hell with poetry?'

The sequence of nine headings for the anthology is interesting, leading from 'Rooted in nature', through 'Changing the landscape', 'Killing the wildlife', 'Unbalance of nature', 'Loss and persistence', and 'The great web' to 'Exploitation', 'Force of nature' finally to 'Natural Disasters' which include nuclear ones. '*Earth Shattering* ends with planetary catastrophe and Eco-Armageddon,' says Astley unapologetically. The anthology intends, he says, 'to alert and alarm'. This is an interventionist anthology: 'anyone whose resolve is stirred will strengthen the collective call for change.' *Earth Shattering* includes critical extracts from debates about ecopoetry and therefore provides the site for a crucial debate about what ecopoetics could and should be.

So this anthology has raised for me the following questions to which some answers will be found within this edition of *MPT*:

1. Do we need a new kind of poetry for our times?
2. Is interventionist poetry a contradiction in terms?
3. Should ecopoetry be positioned as ecopolitics?
4. Should ecopoetry be focussing on an 'alert and alarm', or on sustainable ecotopias, or ways of getting there – the portentous, or the possible, or the practical?
5. What makes good ecopoetry?
6. In what exemplars do we recognise it?
7. What are the weaknesses we are wary of anyway?
8. Does artistic quality of writing have to be compromised to accommodate urgently needed data such as scientific content?

9. For example, can percentages ever be used in poetry successfully?
10. Do we need a new aesthetics, as our criteria for judging the quality of ecopoetry are changed by the urgency of our current needs?

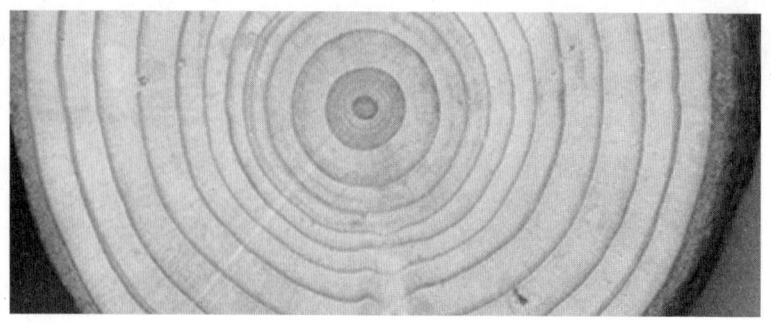

Pauline Stainer
Six poems

In praise of flying squirrels

Understatement is not their thing
as they graze the barbaric blue
like unauthorised gods

theirs is the middle kingdom
below swift and sickle moon,
small drama, with deep focus

their bleached bellies
cross-bandaged
in the diagonal light

until at dusk
the stars let slip
another electric circus.

Hares at dusk

They give nothing away
in the lesser dark,
the varying hares

their focus
the shuttered blues
between pasture and late snow.

It is mesmerising
how many things go missing
at the witching hour

only a waterworn moon
and the rippling machinery
of the moment

still holding the light.

The Sounding

It was dumb-show,
a bird's wing protruding
from the organ-pipe
between stiff sheaves
of lilies

but the stopped note –
that moment
when memory
takes a slip of time
and strikes it

was its far cry
a god's mouth
rinsed out
with sulphur,
tamarisk

or simply
how death
the nightingale
once wintered in your throat?

Overwintering

Light and its loss.
Each day
a guessing game,
the snow which fell
several centuries ago
everything and nothing.

Thaw
almost within earshot,
sigh of an axe
in its antler-sleeve,
passwords pronounced
by the dead

a girl buried
with flowering yarrow
and three crab-apples,
as if her breasts
were still giddy
with milk

the vanishing point
a wave of cherry blossom
moving through memory
until we are dazed
by the slow pollen
the gradual dazzle.

Our Lady of the dry tree

Fifteenth century —
mother and child
embraced by thorns
on a tiny oak panel.

No electric diadems —
but they burn
in the difficult light
as if their barren tree
were still vivid
with sap.

Peregrini

Solitary, devout,
they settle on remote islands
knowing patience is deeper
over great moss.

Occasionally, between
the lapsed psalms
and floating sweet grass
they hear muffled depth-charges

as if the horizons
they jettisoned
for darkening fugues
of salt and sleet

begin to close
on their snow-axed light
and they detect
voice-overs

telling
how the atolls
glow with pollution
and perfect vaccines.

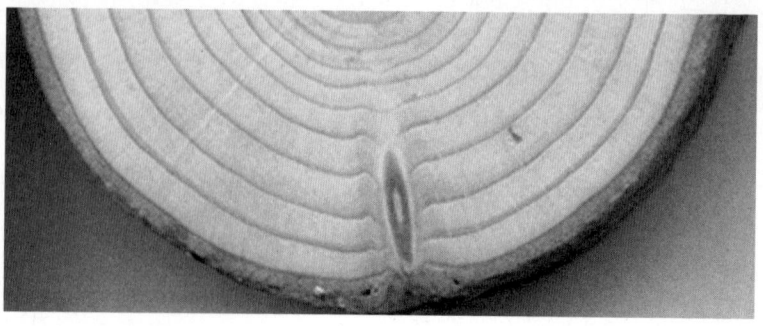

Jeff Nosbaum
'Cape Weavers'

'Cape Weavers' is not a translation or version as such, except insofar as it represents my attempt to translate simultaneously a Cape weaver's nest and a Cape weaver's weaving of that nest. Also, I am generally happy for my poems to be read in any direction a reader may care to read them, but I'll note that, for me, this poem works best if you start in the centre and follow the figure of eight around. I realise this means that technically the poem never ends (which is a lot to ask of a reader), but I usually stop when I run out of breath.

Cape Weavers
Settler's Inn, Grahamstown

```
                in & out
    an asp      they go
from a basket   into a cocoon
   to steal     to a perch
a bright strip  to a wreath, in
   of green         branch, in
from a neighbour    twine &
that hangs          & grass &
from a beak         of leaf
— serpentine —  their threads
& back          weavers spin
thru the hole   the cape
to fill         another
another hole    of one
            in & out
  where      of one
    branches of Africa  another
   cacophonous     the cape
   not like these weavers wend
   of northerly trees their way,
   thru the forests   chattering
   that flit          chirrups
   the whistles       rattling
   to follow      tantrums, songs
   we've crafted  more percussive
   the woodwinds  than the avian
   pit from       sounds that
     the orchestra       fly
            all about
```

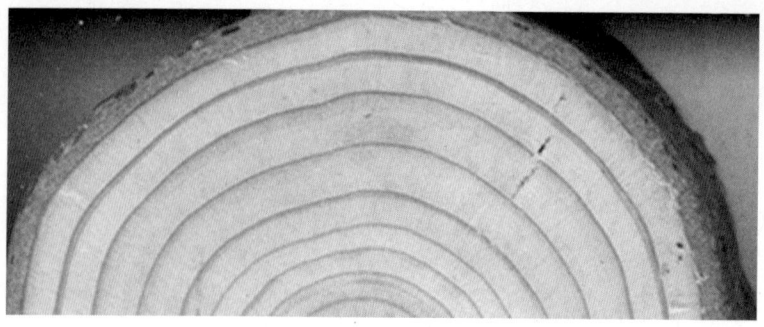

Siriol Troup
Three poems

Snow in April

And what if this were the last snow ever, this white dream
dropping from the sky in British Summer Time –
freak April flurries that fool the leafing trees,
the unsuspecting garden chairs?

Would you rush out to capture muffled streets
and feathered lawns, soft-topped cars, fresh-iced
gingerbread houses, cast your fallen angels
on a pristine continent, try to take in once and for all

the miracle of snowflakes tenderly reforming your world
so years from now there'll be a softness to fall back on
when, lifting your head from the page, you catch

the whitebeam's melting buds beyond the pane
and with a shivered spine, a chill on your tongue,
finally understand you won't see snow again?

Rumours of Rain

On good days we sweat like drains, remembering
slugs and streams, Gore-tex and gutters,
archaic morphemes: *drizzle, paddle, drown.*

We pin our hopes on mesospheric clouds.
Our rods leap up at windscreen wipers, rusty taps,
the gargle of hosepipes languishing in sheds.

We find ourselves acclimatized to hell
but to dream is to lose our bearings, to wake
with frogs in our throats, duck-weed under our nails.

We'd ditch the future for a scabby peach or plum.
There's talk of massacres kicked off by sunflower oil
and liquid soap. One day the rain will come.

Throw-away

The toaster bought with Green Shield stamps
in 1968 needs servicing, my father tells the man
who's just a boy and says it's not worth spending
time on. But it's charred his crusts for almost
forty years, the smell of carbon clinging to his suit
from train to desk to golden handshake to slow
breakfasts filling up unscheduled hours; it cost
good money in the days when people thought
to fix things when they broke, to mend a plug,
replace a battery, turn a collar, sew a button on.
The boy tells him to bin it. Life's too short.
For under twenty quid he'll get a new one,
Japanese or German, slots for thick or thin,
state-of-the-art, available in white or chrome or red
with neon lights, a shade selector and a tray
to catch the ashes drifting from a world
where goods you fought for saw you to the end
then soldiered on to do your children proud.

Mark Leech
'Oil'
A version of Dante, *Purgatory* canto xix, 1-36

Dante's dream encounter with the Siren is a sudden lurch in the otherwise upward progress of the *Purgatorio*. Standing alone, it captures the nightmarish quality of humankind's addiction to its own destruction – yet at the same time offers some hope of escape. This version was written alongside similar re-imaginings of several Old English poems. Like many translations, it is an experiment in bringing the perspective and authority of a particular text directly to bear on a modern problem, and vice versa, while keeping the framework of the original vision intact.

Oil

When the day had given up the world
to the hard moon, thrashed by Earth
or Saturn, or some other punisher

the hour that prophets foretell the rising
of great stars out east down roads
that flare with falling shells

a woman came staggering to me
eye-pained, foot-bound, hands
yellowed with a cancer.

My gaze upon her membraned flesh
jerked her straight, as from a morgue
her tongue slopping free

her body stiff like one about to fall.
Her face washed in a flood of colour –
some lust, or blood, had burst its banks.

So her story was released, and she
keened a note that held me closer
than any prayer-built hope:

'I the Siren, sweet in my throat,
sweet on the sea, bring crude men
to ruin, spilt on rocks and currents.

Wandering Ulysses was trapped in my slick:
any man who's burned for me is caught –
no engine can undo my grip.'

At her pause a lady, cold, stepped
between us. Her icy breath thinned
the Siren's spell to air, invisible.

'She's got him! He's bending to her lips!'
My guide was closing in, eyes fixed
on her white shroud. He grabbed the Siren

and laid her open, the belly slack,
stinking, choking me, waking me
with poisoned air. My eyes fell

on my guide. 'Three times I've called on you
to wake!' he said. 'Now rise: this path
will take us on to lighter skies.'

Wulf Kirsten
'village'
Translated by Dennis Tomlinson

Wulf Kirsten established his reputation as a poet in the former East Germany and, since the events of 1989-90, he has kept a critical eye on contemporary society in the new German state. He was born in the village of Klipphausen, near Meissen in Saxony, in 1934 and his writing is strongly marked by his rural upbringing. Even in the 1970s, when 'progress' was highly valued by the East German state, he was speaking out against the loss of nature, landscape and the village as it had developed over centuries. 'village' was written in 1974 and published in *Der Bleibaum: Gedichte,* Berlin and Weimar: Aufbau-Verlag, 1977; reprinted in *erdlebenbilder: gedichte aus 50 jahren,* Zürich: Ammann Verlag, 2004.

village

the oversettled settlement,
how it boldly hangs there,
tattered and torn
between the fly-tips
that fritter themselves
from no-place to no-place.
the song the girls sang picking berries –
a shred of memory
in the shrunken forest.
companies clear-felling
in ascending line.
the courses of rivers' lives
relentlessly corrected.
played-out pianos,
soundboards bottom-up.
ground elder's working the pedals.
the mill hopper gets hold of things:
was that a cricket chirruping in the sloe bush?
did the farmer's singing master soar to heaven?
the mill hopper gets hold of words:
brook, mole cricket, foal.
life carried off bit by bit.
the village,
watch it being devoured,
in the end it devours itself;
watch it passing away
against the fragment-wreathed void!
watch it disappearing
into the mill hopper, brick by brick.

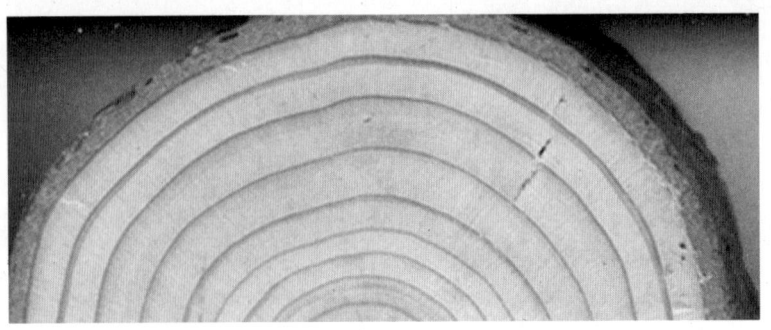

Wulf Kirsten
'Bleak Place, a triptych'
Translated by Stefan Tobler

Wulf Kirsten was born in Klipphausen in 1934, near to Meissen in the German state of Saxony, and now lives in Weimar, where he spent much of his working life as an editor with an East German publishing house. His poetry shows a keen observation of the natural world and our impact on it. The destruction that accompanied East German farm collectivisation is present in his poetry, for example in 'A Feast for the Eyes', published with other of his poems in *MPT* 3/2. He has also researched and written extensively on Buchenwald concentration camp. Kirsten's collected poems, *Erdlebenbilder*, were published in 2004 by Ammann Verlag.

Buchenwald, the German for 'beech wood', is only miles from Weimar, the small city where German culture flourished, particularly in Goethe, Herder and Schiller. Yet it lies on an exposed ridge, where the weather was always much harsher than in Weimar's valley. For this reason, no one had lived on the hilltop before the concentration camp was built there, and the camp prisoners' accounts mention the terrible conditions many times, another torture in addition to the sadism of the camp guards and of many of the *kapos*, the prisoner-overseers, often recruited from the criminal prisoners.

The Ettersberg hilltop was, however, a popular destination for excursions, and a particularly large old oak was known as Goethe's Oak. It was said that he had written the Walpurgis Night scene of *Faust* under it, and that it would last as long as the German Reich. When the Nazis cleared the wood to make way for the camp, it was the only tree left in the barren camp area. Prisoners were hung on it, and the dogs, unable to reach the bodies, tore the bark off the tree. The oak didn't show any immediate signs of change, but in 1942 it had few leaves, and they fell early. The next year it had no leaves, and seeing this gave the inmates hope, remembering what people said about the tree. In August 1944 during an Allied bombing raid on nearby factories, a few bombs fell in the camp. The dead tree caught fire and the prisoners, rushing to put out other fires, let it burn, happy to see Goethe's Oak destroyed.

1
Bleak day in a bleak place, lifted to hilltop,
towards ground a swathe of black clouds,
sheer over quarry and grazing land
the wheezing storm bellows, bites
into wood, jangling and rattling
through the dead's forest, a blizzard
sweeps down at an angle,
how it rips and blows through the leaves
that cover the place of the skulls,
suddenly lifted on high, airworthy
and light: beech wood, Buchenwald weather.

2
Iron hoops on the steep slope,
smashed tin sheeting,
rust-eaten utensils,
scattered wildly in the undergrowth
thriving on clumps of rubble,
dogwood covers the stretch up
as easily, unaided, as I do,
plate halves, bowls,
Rosenthal mark porcelain,
a leather shoe crumbles
before my eyes, up there
barracks, barracks, occupied
by Death's Head units,
all-calculating barbarians,
who scattered out
in wild flight, devils
in hiding, as good honest people
resurrected, peaceable,
never hurt a fly, useful members,
even if without memory.

3
Sea detritus, *soul-darkened the chalk face,*
cut out of the hill, stone-carrier
Poller, his shoulder raw and he
like a ton of lead, up the abrupt slope,
its switchback path, as if *fate's millwheel*
ground him, on stone in the earth names write
the dead, caught in the line of guards' towers,
here Scholem went, there Minister Winterstein,
captive in nature, an endless chain
of names, without any defence,
a grey day, that gives me no rest, no one
else going down these paths for the eye

past leafless growths, starting points
over the edge, treacherous
on limestone, *the ruthless hordes like blown
chaff,* from this shack, on whose outline
I stand, the *kapos* leapt out, thrashed
with shovel handles, until they broke.
Gently rising lines, moss-covered
hill caps, over bodies brought to standstill
in the hauled out quarry, shut down,
as if nothing had happened.

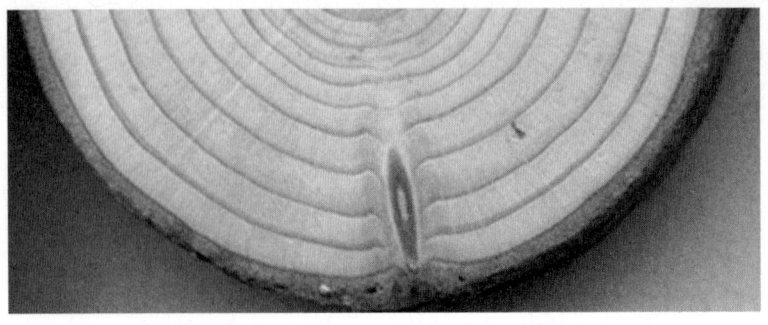

Elisha Porat
Three poems
Translated from the Hebrew by Cindy Eisner

Elisha Porat, a 1996 winner of Israel's Prime Minister's Prize for Literature, has published nineteen volumes of fiction and poetry, in Hebrew, since 1973. His works have appeared in translation in Israel, the United States, Canada, and England.

Bloody Aquifer

In this late spring, in the time before
the first summer fruits, I cruise
the roadways idly.
My mortal eye sees:
stalks of withered hollyhock and clusters of
dill, among the blossoming vegetables.
But with my other eye I
see in your deep basins,
Oh my beloved ravaged land,
blood gathering and draining: from under
the scorching subsoil, your bloody
groundwater surfaces, rises and floods.

My Poems are Wrapped in Darkness

Like a migrant Thai worker I pedal
my bicycle on the village path. Hunched over, dark,
my face covered against the dust. The dogs bark at me,
the bees slam into my forehead, and the scent
of a distant homeland assaults my nostrils.
And like his letters home, silverplating
the sweat of his brow, my poems too are wrapped
with the darkness that covers the land of my longing.

A Small Addendum
to Eilon Cohen

An amateur pilot and a devoted Darwinist crouches
cramped among the controls of a 'flying motorcycle':
fashioning on one knee an astonishing late
addendum to a treatise by Charles Darwin
on a fundamental point of evolution.
His hands, quivering from tension and from inspiration,
smooth the folds of a navigation map
and on its reverse he inscribes, tearing the paper:
Not to the survivors among us is the glory,
but rather to those visionaries
who are loaded like a missile to be shot
far from our filthy planet.
To be shot to a new 'nova',
arriving forcefully on the ground, to create
it all anew. Without looking back,
without longing, and certainly without
useless writers of poetry.

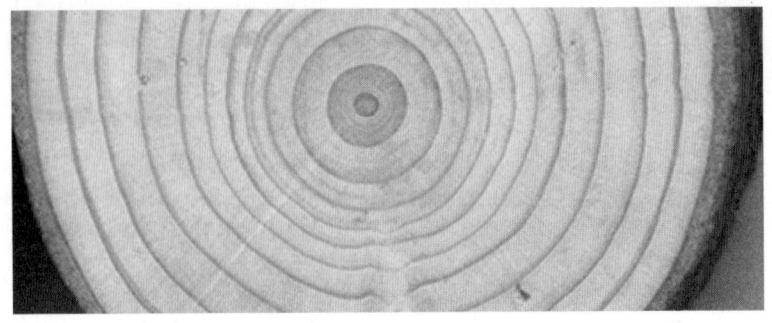

Anne Cluysenaar
Two poems

Echo

It's an exposed spot,
where we stand. From here
the forest can be heard: it shouts
but only if we shout first.

I expect you, step-grandson,
to delight in shouting, but
as I shout and the forest answers
you burst into tears, afraid.

Afraid perhaps of me,
of my voice magnified, thrown
down over both of us,
again and again, from that ridge?

Or of your silence, not
echoed, lost among trees,
among unseen trunks, branches,
roots gripping the stones.

What for me was poetic nicety
is for you the real terror
of a world answering back
from greater and greater distances.

Eels

Glass eels, that in open ocean
passed for glints or ripples,
nose into rainflow freshness.
Their gills flush crimson.

Seeking the bright still cup
of our pond, where swallows dip
to drink, newly visible hearts
beat under see-through skin.

Future years upstream will turn
their skins to brown, then gold,
so that mud-shine conceals them,
and the slimy rims of rocks.

Far off, blue ice is diluting
the Gulf Stream. Their final changes,
big eyes, silver skin, starvation,
may not be enough any more.

Nosing for salt beginnings,
powerful, ready to breed,
to die, they'll retrace the flow,
so long as the flow goes on.

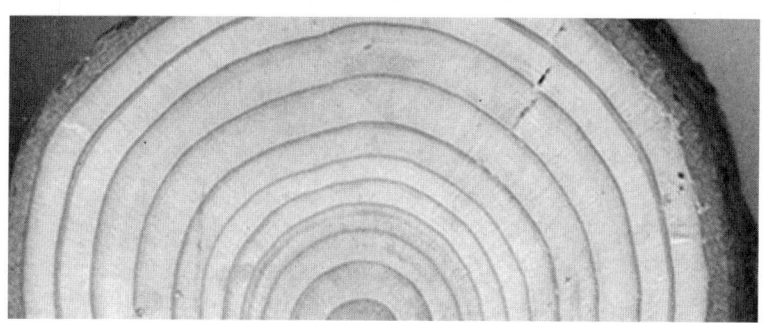

Anna Crowe

The Mysterious Starling
(Aplonis mavornata)

> . . . It seems, just now,
> To be happening so very fast;
> 'Going, Going' by Philip Larkin

. . . *killed while hopping about a tree.*
Emptied of song and spirit to a poverty

of feathered skin, *Aplonis mavornata*,
brown and drab, lies in a drawer

in the British Museum, provenance unknown,
for a hundred years. Until Storrs Olson

tracks down a mention in the poet Byron's
uncle's captain's log, with other extinctions:

the bodies of Liholiho and Kamamalu,
king and queen of Hawaii, whom measles blew

away in London, are being shipped
to Honolulu, where their people's lips

part like a wave around the prow
in a great cry. But now

the *Blonde* sails on to touch at Mauke where,
in the space of just two hours,

Bloxham, ship's naturalist, will shoot a pigeon,
kingfisher, starling, as Captain George Anson,

Lord Byron, borrowing one Maria
Graham's notes—scant and drier

than a dead starling—writes: *killed while hopping
about a tree* . . . The birds were gone, done hopping,

by 1970, when one DT Holyoak,
naturalist, returned to Mauke.

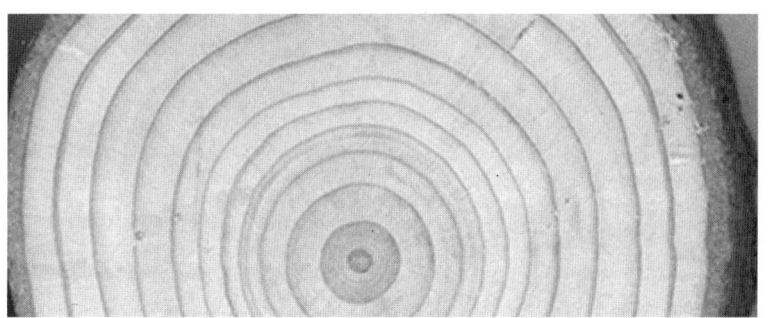

Pedro Serrano
Swallows

Born in Montreal, Canada, in 1947 Pedro Serrano is a Professor in the Faculty of Philosophy and Letters at the National Autonomous University of Mexico. He has published five poetry collections, the latest being *Desplazamientos* (Editorial Candaya, Barcelona 2007), and he co-edited *La Generación del Cordero* (Trilce 2000), an anthology of contemporary British Poetry. His poetry has been widely anthologised and translated, notably in *Reversible Monuments: An Anthology of Contemporary Mexican Poetry*, Copper Canyon Press (Port Townsend, WA) 2002.

He was a founder of the *Cartapacios 'Notebooks'* literature magazine, editor-in-chief of the magazine *Mexico en el Arte 'Mexico in Art,'* and is founder member of the magazine *Fractal*. He is also currently the editor of UNAM's notable poetry publication, *Periódico de Poesía*. Pedro Serrano has translated Shakespeare's *King John* and Matthew Sweeney's *Do Not Throw Stones at this Sign*, and he wrote the libretto for the opera, *Las Marimbas de l'Exil/El Norte in Veracruz* (music by Luc LeMasne).

Serrano studied Spanish literature at Mexico's National Autonomous University (his doctoral thesis was a comparative analysis of the poetry of T.S. Eliot and Octavio Paz) and English literature at the University of London. He was invited to conduct research as part of the Faculty of Philology at the Autonomous

University of Barcelona, Spain and has taught classes in Poetry and Philosophy on the Faculty of Philosophy at the University of Barcelona. He is a member of the Sistema Nacional de Creadores de Mexico.

Swallows

Pinned to the wire like clothes-pegs,
diminutive seagulls made of wood,
lithe and tiny in the brutal force of the blue,
motionless at noon, dropping one after another,
setting in motion clothes, arms, smiles,
with white breasts and black caps, streamlined
wings and in single file, with minimal fuss.
Until all have flown but one,
that perched for a moment and clung to its return,
as though to sketch the lightest of goodbyes,
with morning suddenly an armpit.
The wires remain, the sky never so empty,
like a village wedding on a Sunday,
then nothing.

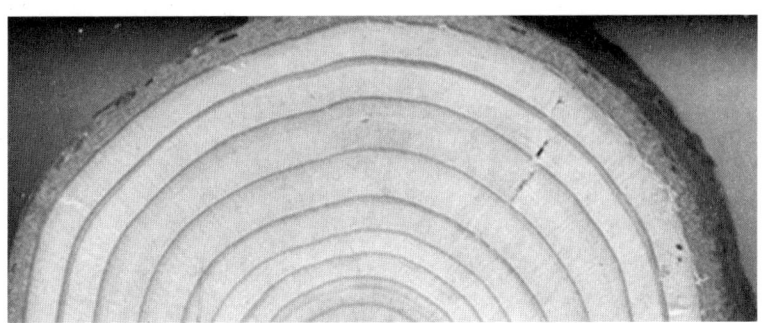

Mangalesh Dabral
Two poems
Translated from Hindi by Sudeep Sen

Mangalesh Dabral (born in 1948) has published five collections of poems in Hindi: *Pahar Par Laltein* (Lantern on Mountain,1981), *Ghar Ka Rasta* (The Way Home, 1981), *Hum Jo Dekhate Hain* (That Which We See, 1995), *Aawaaz Bhi Ek Jagah Hai* (Voice Too is a Place, 2000), *Mujhe Dikha Ek Manushya* (I saw a Human Being, 2008); and three collection of prose: *Ek Baar Iowa* (Once upon Iowa , travel diary, 1996), *Lekhak Ki Roti* (Writer's Bread, cultural essays, 1998), and *Kavi Ka Akelapan* (Poet's Solitude, 2008). His poems have appeared in *Periplus* , *Atlas, Gestures and Signatures, Modern Poetry in Translation, Poetry Review* and *Europa*. His awards include: the Sahitya Akademi Award, Sahityakar Samman, and Pahal Samman. Dabral lives in New Delhi and works with National Book Trust.

For Children, a Letter
(Bachchon ke liye Chitthi)

Dear children, we were of no use to you. You wanted that we spend our precious
time in your play. You wanted that we, in our play,
include you. You wanted that we become innocent like you.

Dear children, we only told you that life is a battleground where
we fight endlessly. It was us who sharpened our arms. We
only prompted war. It was us whose anger and hatred made us blind. Dear
children, we lied to you.

This is a long night – like a tunnel. From here we can see
outside, and its unclear view. We can see killing and lamentation.
Children, we sent you there. Forgive us. We lied to you
by saying life is a battleground.

Dear children, life is a festival where you are spread out like laughter.
Life is a green tree upon which you are perched as fluttering birds.

As some poets have said, life is a tossed-up ball and
you are, surrounding it, a gathered group of restless feet.

Dear children, if this is not so, it ought to be so.

Before Going To Sleep
(Sone Se Pahlay)

Before going to sleep I collect the morning papers
And push away the day's headlines
I don't like to remember the dates of killing and tyranny
I don't want to know with how much bloodshed nations are
   being made
I turn over the pictures
A bridge is collapsing lamentation is rising
A face begging for its lifeline
A man sitting on a chair roaring in laughter

All night will a despot keep staring at me
All night shall I keep seeing displaced people roaming
Moving towards some unknown arid land
All night will my breath suffocate due to earth's rising
   temperature
Will a bazaar keep knocking at my head
Before going to sleep I close my books
Where trees hills buildings people are all drowned in
   black-n-white sorrow
And love looks like a dishevelled nest

Before going to sleep I drive all scary images away
And close the windows
Put out my cigarette slide my slippers under the bed
Before going to sleep I drink a glass of water
And say water you remain around
I take a deep breath
And say air stay here between my lungs and these walls
Before going to sleep I say
Sleep give me at least a nice enough dream.

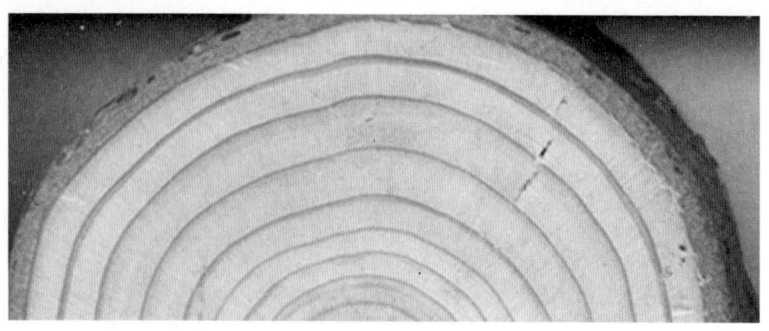

Extending the Territory
20th International Aldeburgh Poetry Festival, 7–9 November 2008

If part of the poet's role is to be an outsider – to reflect their culture, stir things up, challenge people's assumptions – then the two writers in translation coming to Aldeburgh this year are doing a consummate job.

Yi Sha's deceptively informal but resonant narratives have attracted fierce criticism at home and he's been refused permission to give readings outside China on a number of occasions. We first discovered his dissident writing in 2004 (via the Poetry International website) and were immediately surprised and captivated by poems that confound cultural expectation. Four years on, and after effecting a successful Bloodaxe introduction, Aldeburgh will celebrate Yi Sha's first reading in the UK – he'll be accompanied by his Australian translator Simon Patton – and the launch of his first publication in English outside China.

Since 2004, and as part of the packed programme of major readings, craft talks, discussions, lectures, workshops and masterclasses, Aldeburgh has featured 'Close Readings'. These free 15-minute events – in which a poet shares the pleasures of a poem – are threaded throughout the weekend to remind us all just how much a single poem, in *any* language, can communicate. One of this year's six Close Readings will be delivered by Yi Sha, aided by Simon Patton. And Simon will also talk about 'Poetry in China', to flag up some of today's leading Chinese lights and reflect on the experience of translating the language into English.

South Africa's Antjie Krog became famous in the mid-nineties for her radio journalism and her subsequent publication *Country of My Skull* about the Truth and Reconciliation Commission hearings. From her very first collection in 1970, she has tackled race, politics, feminism, sexuality and ageing with uncompromising and ground-breaking candour. Described as the Pablo Neruda of Afrikaans, her poetry is available in Dutch, Italian, French, German, Spanish and Arabic, and she now translates herself into English.

Since 1990, when South Africa's new constitution recognised eleven official languages instead of just English and Afrikaans, Krog's original language has lost nearly all of its power. But she continues to write first in Afrikaans – '. . . the poetic inner life only comes to life in my mother tongue . . . I want the reader/listener to be aware all the time that he or she is busy with somebody that is NOT English.' Increasingly dissatisfied, though, with the quality and choice of her poems in English translations – 'they felt to have been written by someone else' – Krog began to self-translate at the end of the 1980s. And although she is now able to trust her ear more and more in English, she's acutely aware that her own linguistic and cultural identity is in a tumultuous state of flux.

At Aldeburgh, she'll be talking about 'The Afrikaans Tradition', its social and political identity, its musical strengths, and its place in South African culture today. 'I am passionate about translation,' she says. 'I believe that it is crucial for people in a country with such a divided, separated past to translate one another in order to begin to form some kind of coherent and undominated consciousness . . . if we really want to understand where and how we live.'

> 20th Aldeburgh Poetry Festival, 7–9 November 2008
> full details available from www.thepoetrytrust.org
> for a printed programme or further information:
> info@thepoetrytrust.org or 01986 835950

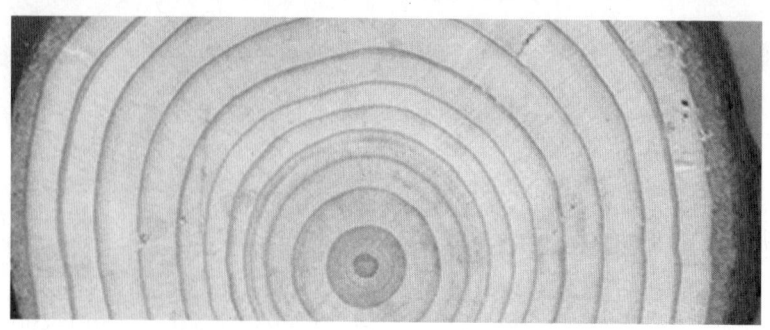

Yi Sha
Five poems
Translated by Simon Patton and Tao Naikan

Yi Sha is the most controversial Chinese poet of the past twenty years, a member of the extreme avant-garde whose work has changed the face of Chinese poetry. His anti-lyrical poetry is minimal, unadorned, dramatising with facts, not painting emotional pictures, in plain, colloquial language. His poems present pared-down descriptions of seemingly banal incidents, or dramatic incidents described in an ironically banal manner.

Born in the southern Chinese city of Chengdu in 1966 three days after the start of the Cultural Revolution, he grew up in the Maoist era. He came to prominence as a writer in the 1990s, publishing fiction and essays as well as poetry, all of which have been criticised, attacked and even reviled by detractors including many fellow writers. No Chinese poet before him has come under such concentrated attack.

Although Yi Sha is a literature professor, his poetry is anti-academic in flavour and has never been accepted in the official Chinese literary mainstream. He has refused to join any official Chinese writers organisation, which has made him a non-official poet, and his writing has been imitated by still younger poets. Those who condemn Yi Sha say he has damaged the Chinese poetic tradition, while his admirers believe that he has given forceful expression to the current realities of China and extended the appeal of poetry to new audiences. His poetry has been translated into several languages, but he has been refused permission to give readings outside China on a number of occasions. His *Selected Short Poems* was published in a bilingual Chinese-English edition in Hong Kong in 2003. *Starve the Poets!* (Bloodaxe Books, 2008), his first English publication outside China, will be launched at Aldeburgh Poetry Festival in November.

At the Zoo

I haven't been to this zoo for 18 years
On this visit here today
I've brought my young son along to see
that there are other creatures on this planet besides us humans
In the tiger enclosure the animal here now
is not the one I knew 18 years ago
That was this one's mother
It died one summer ten years ago
That's not important
All my son needs to know
is that it's a tiger
Later, when it growls
my son starts bawling
so I take him away
to look at the spotted deer
Because I coax it
with a handful of grass
it pushes its muzzle

up against the railing
As it does this
my fearless son grabs at its head
with his tiny fingers
and pokes it viciously in the eyes
                                [1996]

Hong Kong 1997

When you were poor
you sold off your own child

As his mother
you couldn't bring yourself to say
he'd been captured by bandits

But now he's back
The child you sold off
with a straw 'for sale' sign on his head
is back

A smart gentleman
wearing a Western-style suit and leather shoes
now sits opposite you
his glossy hair slicked back, his chin shaved

I seem to hear him say:
'I am now just a guest
in my parent's home'
                                [1997]

Dumplings

Even on the last day of the lunar year
he and his father were hard at work
labouring in the fields from dawn to dusk
That is the reason why
he has such a clear recollection of the very last sunset
of the Year of the Snake
Back home
his mother served up a meal
of steaming hot dumplings
After dinner he went straight to bed
because he and his father
had to go back into the fields again the following day
This he had to do
because the university fees he needed to pay each year
came (and could only come)
from tilling the soil

A university student
from a village
recounted to everyone present
how he spent his New Year's Eve
as an exercise in oral presentation skills
in my class
In the five minutes he took to tell his story
his delivery was smooth, steady
his tone was detached
It was only when he got
to the word 'dumplings'
that a smile crept over his face
                              [2002]

News of SARS

A plague has come
The virus prevails everywhere
The really worrying thing is that
people die every day
Yesterday our national TV
telecast a piece of news
which claimed that
because of timely prevention
and the adoption of appropriate measures
the animals
in the zoo
were all safe
and had not been infected
They lived well
I kept my cool
Not that I didn't hear the news
but I was able
to do the sums:
the little lives of these animals
were worth more
than those of people

[2003]

China's Tomb Sweeping Day

Maybe because we're not in the habit
of standing before God
we cannot stand
before the grave of departed loved ones
heads hung in silence
muttering prayers
That's how we are, we Chinese
We're not stuck up –
we're relaxed
On Tomb Sweeping Day
the weather having fined after rain
I sat with the rest of my family
around the grave of my ancestors
built in the shape of a courtyard
It was like sitting down to a special dinner at home
We talked about this and that quite naturally
as if the dead were still with us
and could hear what we said
and answer us with their silences
The fruit we offered them
was, in the end, eaten by the children
They say this brings good luck

For the Chinese
Tomb Sweeping Day is a holiday
a chance to get out of the city and enjoy the spring scenery
together with the ghosts and spirits of the dead
who inhabit these hills and fields
      [2005]

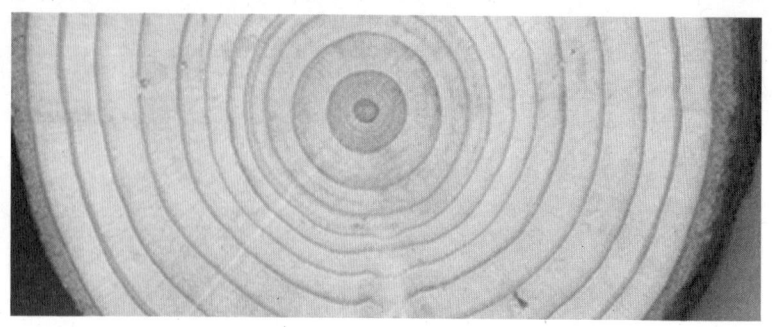

Antjie Krog
'the unhomely'
Translated out of Afrikaans by the author

Antjie Krog was born on a farm in the Orange Free State, South Africa in 1952. She lives in Cape Town where she is a Professor Extraordinary at the University of the Western Cape. Writing in Afrikaans as well as English, she has won every major South African literary prize. She has also received the Sunday Times Alan Paton Award and was honoured by the Hiroshima Peace Foundation. She has published eleven collections of poems – most recently *Body Bereft* (2006) – as well as translations and non-fiction, most notably *Country of My Skull*, an account of the hearings of the Truth and Reconciliation Commission.

the unhomely

the lane is a spine
the lane constructs itself up the hill
the lane exudes its fragrance with turpentine and pine, with
    balm
                mulberry and spirals of pencil-blue cedars
and being from neither here nor there, she cannot begin to
    know
how blue green is
how olive the purple
how motionless the cypresses and the folds of their capes
                as lightning sears the sky
and the earth rumbles back on the brink of grief

the lane is a castle
the lane is the only way to the castle
the lane intensifies into sweet chestnut and sage, white
    willow
                sycamore and ash
and she from the marginals of the world, is not there to feel
how the broom rustles its fragrant earlobes
how a hue of saffron glides towards those talking in the
    twilight
how alive the dark is, how grainy the bolt
how bloody the wingtips of swallows flash against the
    morning sun
how cold a pear sings in a saucer on a table of granite
the very moment the castle sinks into a roaring gas-flame of
    midday trees

the lane shimmers like a knight
the lane marches up the slope
the lane preserves itself with maple, with oak, with lucern
                              buckthorn and elm
the lane feels the only decipherer of the abandonment of
   swifts
of how the barn owl lets its lonely chisel sounds slip
of how sparrows snip and snip deeper into gathered shrouds
   of dew
how milk thistle and chicory bleed blue butterflies
                              from their stems in the lane
how cicadas burnish the black figs
of how, from hand to hand, an ice-blue shoulder slides from
   the cross
and the unhomely fade into frescoes

the lane holds to the word: reign
the lane forms the self through the self
the lane knows that generations of Ranieris are listening
   down the stone passages to whose feet sound on the gravel
from beyond the lane she knows the lines are drawn
but is unaware whether its by bones lying around
                              in cupboards like weapons
or by dogs furiously storming towards the mauve smear of a
   hare
or the bursting of pheasants into flecked whirring buttons
or the devastating blonde scabs of recently mowed fields
smouldering behind the lane where some notes drift

the lane endures the sun
the lane absorbs all water all sap all power
the lane is a survivor – the cedars grow their hard silver
   tassels
the gnats rise like sleaze to the iron bars and deep slit
   windows
                           of the stone walls
but the lane, oh, the lane is impenetrable
as the group, leaning towards each other
                           with their worn-out hearts, knows
that among the concepts they discuss, she's not even a shadow
she who undertook never to be sad in this world
is learning that beyond this beyond is another beyond
and beyond that, always, radiantly: the lane

Antjie Krog (2008)

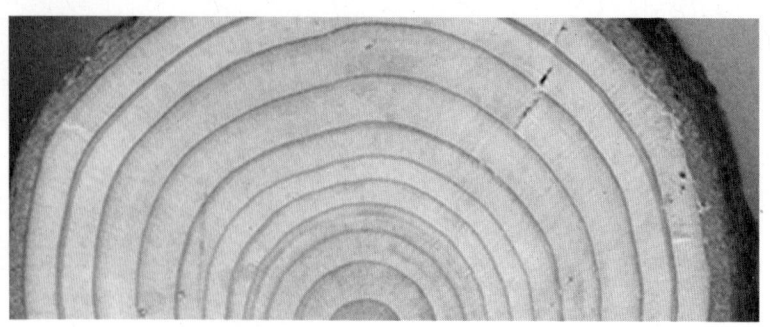

Farzaneh Khojandi
Two poems
Translated by Jo Shapcott

Born in the remote Khojand province of Tajikistan in 1960, Farzaneh Khojandi is widely regarded as the most exciting woman poet writing in Persian (Farsi, Tajik) today and has a huge following in Iran and Afghanistan as well as in Tajikistan, where she is simply regarded as the country's foremost living writer. Her frequently playful and witty poetry draws on the rich tradition of Persian literature in an often subversive and humorous way. Although the Tajik community in the UK is a very small one, there are many Farsi speakers from Iran and Afghanistan resident here, a significant proportion of whom are highly educated and deeply interested in poetry.

Behind the Mass of Green

When the message came with a smile
that summer was coming,
men, sloshing their way
through puddles of muddy water,
carried on oblivious.
But the roses felt the warm kiss
of summer on their necks.

Chicks roared inside cracking shells,
plums blushed with excitement.
My mother lugged our winter clothes
out of the chest of drawers
and spread them in the sun.
I pulled my heart out of my breast,
and laid it in the sun as well,
my heart, smelling of frost, and musty winter.

Listen, from now on, my heart is married to the sun.
While you draw the curtains over it all,
and fall into mid-morning naps,
I make love with the sun.
I'm certain this love is my virtue but maybe it's the
    sun's sin –
because someone hurt me, recently,
someone with a ridiculous laugh,
which broke into the quiet night,
got my name so drunk even street girls shouted it.
Look. There is someone behind this mass of green.
Someone whose eyes, right from the beginning of creation
until this moment, saved faith and love.

Someone whose breath is the astonishment of Jesus,
someone whose touch is a loan from Moses,
someone whose voice veils the song of eclipses,
someone who is seated in the palm of knowledge
and in whose hands the half-apple
waits for sweet lips, someone
who has blessed horizons with dust from his feet.
Yes, behind this mass of green there is someone,
and for him I have come back to life.

A Nightingale in the Cage of my Breast

In this leafy orchard is a nightingale,
a nightingale whose songs are the dawn
and take me into the light,
to the mountains of legendary Farhad,
and to the place where mad Majnun talks to the raven:
'Hello gorgeous!' And to that lucky cave,
luminous with solitude, basking in gold,
and to a paradise where Adam and Eve stare at a wheat grain:
'Shall we taste it or not?' If I were Eve, I wouldn't taste it.
Thank goodness I'm not Eve or else mankind
would never forgive me for not sinning.
O tiny, miraculous wheat grain, O tiny apple of amazement,
O simple beginnings of myself.
There is a nightingale who sings my see-through thoughts,
sings back to the beginnings of memory.
There is a nightingale flying out of the cage of my breast;
it's chirping now at the edge of morning.
I am leaving; I am leaving, my friend.
You have to step into life, spread your existence,
you must hurry,

you must bring to Farhad in the story,
the good news about Shirin, his beloved,
you must enter Zoroaster's cave
and taste the light.
To taste the wheat grain of paradise – or not? O . . .
I am leaving, I am leaving at last:
my friend, open your heart for me.

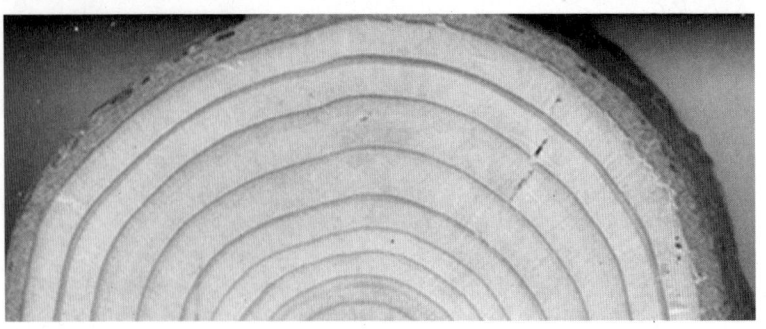

Rose Scooler
'Mica Parade'
Translated by Sibyl Ruth

Rose Scooler was born in 1881, in East Prussia. When she was in her early teens the family moved to Berlin. After a year in Switzerland, Rose became engaged to Sidney Scooler, the son of family friends. The marriage took place shortly before Rose's eighteenth birthday.

Sidney, who was considerably older than his wife, owned a cardboard factory in Porschendorf, near Pirna, in Saxony. The couple had two sons, Werner and Walter, who ran the factory after Sidney died in 1928. It was a flourishing concern. However, in 1938 the business was 'aryanised' – taken over at the price of about 10% of its actual value.

Werner then moved to Dresden. But in 1941 he was taken first to Riga, and from there to Auschwitz. Walter (who had obtained false papers stating he had some Aryan blood) moved to Berlin with Rose. Eventually he was drafted into a forced labour unit attached to the army.

Once she was no longer with Walter, Rose's position became precarious. She was transported to Theresienstadt in January 1944, and worked in the camp's 'home' for the elderly, and later in a workshop splitting mica. It was here she composed and memorised poems as a way of enduring long, monotonous and long shifts. But this labour saved her life. Mica was used in the making of planes; those who prepared it were spared deportation. Rose Scooler was one of the relatively small number of inmates still alive when the camp was liberated in May 1945.

Subsequently Rose spent two years in a Displaced Persons Camp in Bavaria. Then, after a short period in England, she joined Walter in the U.S.A.

Rose lived to the age of 103, and did voluntary work until her late nineties. Her Theresienstadt poems were discovered after Walter died in 2006.

Mica Parade

The Bosses Come First

They enter with measured steps, pacing
down the middle of our workshop. Aristocrats
whose foreheads are arranged in serious folds
– far too busy to think of taking off their hats.
Just watch them striding towards the office . . .
They don't want to award any of us the bare
politeness of a greeting. Instead we have the usual
flickering looks from side to side. Somewhere
a jacket hasn't been hung on its appointed hook –
'For Heaven's sake. Get that wretched thing out
of here!' It's time now to troop off for the low-down
on the latest issue they can complain about.
Soon enough they'll return, thin smiles pinned
to their faces, sitting as judge and jury on our crime.
'Production levels are hanging on a knife edge,
so output must be raised in the shortest time
possible. The other section makes its target

without trouble – which, given that everyone's got
the highest quality materials to work with,
is hardly surprising. Really, we're not asking a lot
from you. Furthermore inmates must now vacate
the premises as soon as their shift is done,
departing in a single orderly group. There will be
no exceptions to this regulation. Anyone
who tries taking the law into their own hands
is certain to find herself under lock and key.'
This is the way they like to hurl their thunderbolts.
Don't our bosses rule creation brilliantly?

Secondly, the Supervisors

They have to be here there and everywhere, trying
to make sure the whole team works happily
together. It's quite a job. Yet they manage somehow,
shouldering this heavy load with dignity
and pride. Though with a thousand and one things to do
it's impossible for them to have a moment's rest.
A woman can't unwind when she must be ready
to dash off without notice, bagging all the best
material for the group under her care
so their output will be commended as first-rate.
Yes, Output is at the forefront of our minds.
You'll hear the word constantly. There is no escape.
Which is why the supervisors often split mica
alongside the girls and the older women.
It is why they'll fish in the crates to get rid of
the fragments that are no good for splitting.
Why they lend a hand grading the material
and check the stuff that's been rejected. If any
piece does look usable, it will be reclaimed
in order not to squander a single penny.
Because Profit is just as important as Output

in this place. We accept that Profit holds sway.
So when our ladies get summoned to a meeting
we expect that they'll head back without delay
afterwards, keen to instruct an attentive audience
about the new requirements of the powers that be.
Mind you, these aren't the only weighty matters
which our workshop supervisors are obliged to see
to. For every team member, whatever her age,
depends on having a mother figure who knows
the exact sorts of food that are available
and the times when the showers open and close.
A person who is able to steer her charges through
personal crises. Who's aware of what's happening
round the camp – good and bad – including the latest
juicy gossip. Who, in a practical case, will do
what she can to help. So if you want anything
at all, just ask. Our supervisors are the greatest!

Last But Not Least, the Approach of the Mica Women

Here they come. The monstrous regiment gets closer.
A whole army, you might have thought
seeing the lot of them, crammed shoulder to shoulder
and jostling one another. No one escapes the juggernaut
as it rolls past. Wherever you look – left, right,
behind, in front – it's mica women that you see.
Some taking their time. Some fast-paced,
running along in couples or little groups of three.
They gallop down the narrow lanes,
worried they might be late. The others couldn't care
less. They dawdle along, determined to make the most
of an opportunity to enjoy some fresh air
and sunshine. The younger ones with a spring
in their step. Their short skirts dance, swerve
in the breeze. They have applied red lipstick

and each eyebrow has been plucked to a neat curve
Although nobody's done detox or been on a diet,
they've all got the most fantastic figures.
Look down and you'll glimpse ankles – slim or thick,
big or small – in stockings of assorted colours,
set off by military boots. (For those seeking alternatives
try galoshes, clogs or sandals.) And with some girls
who haven't thought to bother with a hat, the wind
is turning mischievous: it messes up their curls.
Even if they opted for a headscarf, turban or cap,
the point is every single one of them looks fetching.
The sheer variety of costumes deserves acclaim.
First and foremost an honourable mention
must go to the maturer ladies, with their own range
of style choices. (Mainly they are modelling slacks.)
To sum up, it is an eye-opening parade of coats
and dresses that's processing towards the barracks,
a truly remarkable kaleidoscope of colour.
Very shortly they'll be reaching their destination,
so check out their accessories now. Those chic handbags
woven out of string. Aren't they the height of fashion?
Once they are through the front door, out of sight,
they'll stop for a snack. Because a morsel to eat
is vital. In today's harsh world, a woman needs
something to lift her spirits and keep her temper sweet.
Friends and neighbours all settle down to a session
trading the latest bits of gossip. Whatever's
been going on, they need to know the juicy details.
Hours have passed since their last get-together!
But one by one people are becoming fidgety.
They feel guilty, almost . . . In any event, it is about
time to knuckle down: there's a good deal to be done.
Each one's thinking, 'Today I'd really better go flat out,
as I wouldn't like to be saddled with the blame
for landing all my group in serious trouble.
Having to work late would be a catastrophe.

So I shall have to concentrate. And be responsible.
Maybe this time I'll even manage to hit our target
and have a good 300 grammes at the end of the day.
Only this batch of material is rubbish. Besides the board
is all wrong. Plus my blade doesn't cut the right way.'
Overcoming so many obstacles, the work of splitting starts.
Because our mica-women are real masters of their craft!

Tomas Venclova
Three poems
Translated by Ellen Hinsey

Tomas Venclova (1937) was born in Klaipeda, Lithuania. He graduated from Vilnius University in 1960. From 1956 on, Venclova took part in the Lithuanian and Soviet dissident movements, making friends with Joseph Brodsky, Natalia Gorbanevskaya, and other participants in the Soviet underground. Venclova was one of the five founding members of the Lithuanian Helsinki group, and in 1977 he emigrated. Since 1985, he has taught Russian and Polish literature, as well as Lithuanian language, at Yale University. His published works include volumes of poetry, criticism, literary biography, conversations and works on Vilnius. He has been the recipient of numerous awards including the Lithuanian National Prize in 2000, the 2002 Prize of Two Nations, which he received jointly with Czeslaw Milosz, the 2005 Jotvingiai Prize, and the New Culture of New Europe Prize, 2005.

Arrival in Atlantis

On the mud promontory is a ghostly depot.
The sailors don't care what country has capsized,
above all, in these days after a drawn-out
war that's left their empire fragmented.

What is left of the hotel's canteen is the view.
Motorboats list and turn. Coming winter,
framed by curtains, is darker than the window—
veiled by cement and grey-clay spattered.

The red beacon, as before, is solidly squat,
but barely perceptible are the fortress's contours.
Seagulls scuffle on the pier, are more stalwart
than cast iron, concrete: above all, ourselves.

Stand still, close your eyes. A traveller's steps
press into backstreets' sand. Eyesight has failed.
We will never meet again. Wherever one turns
one sees the airless bay and the epoch's end.

Thistle, *linnaea borealis*, goat weed.
The wet sheen of metal, riddled with holes.
We sense each other, like Almighty God—
from opposite sides of the abyss: far, yet close.

On the sea's threshold where shallows erode,
the darkish strip of the fairway disappears
like black crepe. But under my hands, poverty
November, grammar and flame still flicker.

Discipline and Punish. A Visit to the Detention Centre IZ-45/1

'And I pray not for myself alone . . .' Anna Akhmatova

It's easier to survive in here than before.
Problems are the same outside: AIDS, TB.
Bromine mixed in gruel somewhat quells
sperm's rage, when outside one happens to
see the contours of female visitors' calves,
as the guards are indulging in Baltika beer.

Words no longer mean the same, the town
roars—divided into two, near the red wall.
A cluster of clouds, a continent behind your
back. When the wind lifts they say a paper
scrap sometimes reaches the other shore,

though more often falls on passing barges—
or simply, onto the flickering ultramarine.
Still, a sign to the morning, algae, nature.
In a cell: six men, not twenty, as before.

A church dome. Beyond, a streetcar's route.
The blind brick wall has learned the slang
of skinheads. Was it far in those days—?
From neglected gardens, decaying columns
down the avenue, disfigured by modernity,

over the bridge's desert, along two streets.
July heat. The deafening rustle of leaves—
blood beats in the veins at a regular rate.
It has been years since the silhouettes of
friends or enemies showed in windowpanes.

Clearings, empty spaces. An émigré felled
on stage in Berlin by a madman's bullet,
leaving behind a son: an uncommon destiny.
A proud, nearsighted poet (whose memory
will be preserved in a field near Magadan);

even the other, who would be born later—
the long road and the polar night over
the Yenisei prepare themselves for him,
(and the Neva and Neman and the river
without a name in Charon's kingdom).

And others who were sure there existed
unfettered air and another life. Here it is:
beyond the gates sparrows scurry about.
A steam boat bellows. We inherit the earth.
Though this is probably small consolation.

Homage to Shqiperia
– *Shqiperia, Albania*

Survey the amphitheatre's ruined hemisphere,
the rocky semicircle—its spokes like pauses
in a monologue. The stage is nearly ideal.
The sponger from the cleverest comedy by Plautus
waves his hand at us. Once Epidamnos was here—
in this poor country, now excessively real.

Our memento: a paper entry, thumbed threadbare,
with a mountain's contour, two words: *pesë lekë*,
and a black locomotive that seems to exist only
on bills. And the rest—windows gaping empty,
rank straw on pavement, the shadow of a bunker
by the coarse, red-haired spine of a donkey.

Phlegethon blazes up in a leeward hollow,
where armed, naked slopes pound water's reflection.
If one were to imagine Europe as a solar system
(oscillating planets, harmonic bonds of constellations),
this country would then be scorching Pluto
whose position is silence and abandon.

One would rather be where one is not, again
I recall this proverb. Here, pomegranates aren't mature,
but the grenades are overripe. I have outlived
three dictators. From exile's safe distance, three more.
But this local version was far worse than
the others combined. I'd even say he slammed

the door shut to the otherworld. Glass grinds
underfoot. A machine gun's slit is like a rotten socket
in a Martian's skull. Networks of bunkers were
dug in limestone, as if posterity needed to be instructed
that there would never again be hell or paradise,
air or water, but only, and at best, fire.

Near sunset, against its will, smell's keen faculty
detects the odour of rats, rubbish, rakia.
Under a veil of ash, a constellation starts to stir—
the way dead white acanthus leaves shake,
the way emptiness drones! It draws its weight from bodies
and then ripens slowly in the atmosphere.

On the dry marble, fruit rinds glow white,
and the ancient comic's contour faintly appears
in tobacco smoke. In my sleep, I hear declaimed:
'*Panta rhei* comes to where stagnation was before—
as to which is better, not even God can predict.
It's a dollar for the wine—two for the aphorism.'

Peace, Poetry and Palestine

An evening of poetry dedicated to Palestine, held at Ustinov College, Durham, on 23rd April 2008. This event was hosted for *MPT* by Durham Palestine Education Trust. There was music from Firas Kirala, and readings from the Spring issue of *MPT*, *Palestine*.

David Constantine

Firas Kirala (Oud)

Mahmoud Darwish (1941–2008)

We published a long extract from Darwish's *A State of Siege* (translated by Sarah Maguire and Sabry Hafez) in 'Introductions', the first issue of *MPT* under our editorship. It seemed a particular privilege to begin like that. Then with two equally abundant poems, 'Mural' (translated by Rema Hammami and John Berger) and 'Like a Hand Tattoo' (translated by Fady Joudah), he made a vital contribution to our Palestine issue (3/9). We read from his work in Durham, to Palestinian students and their friends and supporters. His death earlier this year is a terrible loss. Truly, he was a writer his people and the whole world needed.

David and Helen Constantine

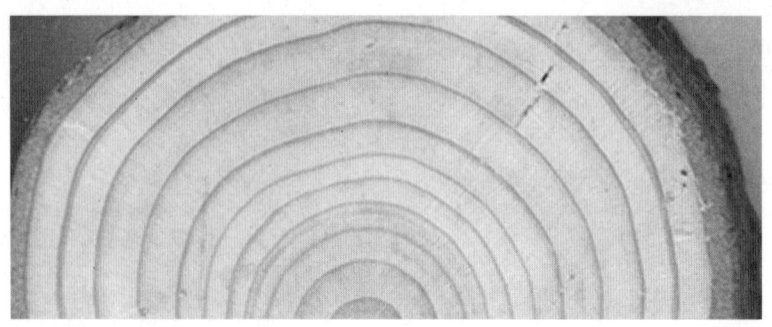

Franz Hodjak
Six poems
Translated by Peter Oram

Franz Hodjak was born in 1944 in Hermannstadt (Sibiu), Romania, and studied German and Romanian language and literature in Klausenburg, where he subsequently worked as a proofreader for the publishing house Dacia. During the following years he became one of the most notable of a number of writers living and working in the largely German-speaking region of Siebenbürgen, and published his first volumes of poetry. In 1992, after long struggles with the censorship practices of the Ceaucescu regime, he moved to Germany, settling finally in Usingen, Hessen. Both his prose and his poetry deal principally either with the confrontation of the free individual with a restrictive and repressive environment, or else with the fate and identity problems of the exile. His poetry is coolly lucid and concise, and expresses a great sense of loss without allowing itself the indulgence of self-pity. His earlier works use clear imagery and are immediately accessible; in later works the language becomes more elliptic and the syntax more fragmented.

Hodjak's publications include the poetry collections: *Sehnsucht nach Feigenschnaps* (Aufbau Verlag 1988); *Siebenbürgische Sprechübung* (1990), *Landverlust* (1993), *Ankunft Konjunktiv* (1997) (all with Suhrkamp Verlag). His published novels include *Grenzsteine* (1995) and *Ein Koffer voller Sand* (2003).

Franz Hodjak has won numerous prizes and awards for his work, among them the Nikolaus Lenau Prize, Heinrich Heine Stipendium, Hermann Hesse Stipendium and the award of honour for the Andreas Gryphius Prize.

how i choose my words

there are still places left
where no one can set up boundaries

where beyond a fence of snow there breathes
another untrodden country

where fires beckon you into strange places
and equip you with wings

where there's no customs office building
of pretexts prefabrications

where behind walls the silence
passes on its tapped-out messages

where the night is darker
by one degree of freedom

in this way i enter into words
this much room to move i need

room to move

the freedom
that each day
grants us
room to move
is exactly the same size as
the room to move
that we grant
each day
to freedom

sărmăşel, klausenburg

faced with this strange earth unexpectedly gripped
by all its incomprehensibility: darkness
drifts towards us
out of this peaceful grass that's all around
on this remote hillock
beneath these free skies (which
it has to be said were not always so free)

suddenly nothing is heavier
than the mud
that clings to our shoes –

forty villagers simply
buried alive in there: one-off
resettlement of an entire village
out of the year nineteen-forty-four
into forever

the obligatory minute of silence
outgrows itself
into enduring reflection: a human being
can't help but become more human
in the face of such inhumanity

for some visitors however
the high perimeter fence separates
much too strictly
innocence from guilt

epitaph
for the vietnamese village
song-my

landscape of funnels through which death flows
like blindfolds clouds ascend
the sun ignited by incandescent timber
                                                    stares like an eye
metal and stone flee deeper into their own hardness
only the wind continues on its way as dumb witness
these bamboo huts may have been poor but even in
the smallest room there was once
room enough for peace

sarmizegetusa

the way up there cat-brained loneliness
unexpected suspicious
behind gardens houses graves
the clearing
randomly gathered and assembled bones
of faded columns porticos slabs
with inscriptions worthy deeds
astonishing words of wisdom
well preserved among the dust of decay
layers of artfully laid mosaic
probably from the basilica
granite paved streets
on the vain flight from transience
indecipherable fragments fortifications
a chaos of mossy masonry
in the folds and masks still the shock
at the onslaught of dark hordes:

Rome's eastern defences
a heap of loose stones
whose sole support was that they in turn supported

(faced with this place Ovid might have wondered:
what is it that drives history
forward: the courage of the victor, or that
of the vanquished?)

still life

nail to hang a saxon jug
a motto to hide a pair of nakednesses
a broken spinning wheel to serve as smiling sun
a clock to keep things in balance
a soot-stained picture
of a young woman with cranes for Ibycus
a panorama of the Carpathians in an open window

all around the walls lost for words
at the shadows
that things cast
into their own interior

Zsuzsa Beney
Five poems
Translated by George Szirtes

Zsuzsa Beney, Hungarian poet, essayist and surgeon, was born in Budapest in 1930. Her first book of poems, *Tűzföld* (Fire-earth) appeared in 1972 with an introduction by Sándor Weöres, one the greatest Hungarian poets of the century. She produced a book of essays the next year and the first of her two novels in 1974. Her 1993 book of essays, *Szó és csend között*, was published in the UK by Mare's Nest as *Between Sound and Silence*, translated by Mark Griffiths. The essays in it are mainly philosophical and mystical meditations following the death of her husband. Her poems are contemplative, often preoccupied by suffering and the borders of existence and non-existence. She continued as a surgeon to her seventieth birthday. She died in July 2006.

The River
(A folyó)

Through what sluices has it swept
before it finally reached my home
of clay soil and carved its crumbling bed?
Eternity humming from its dark source.

The non-transparent water shows time
only its wrinkled silk surface.
Mirror images of sparkling light.
Waves sliding one under the other.

Broken tiles in the mirror,
cracking, and still another glass,
between was and will be, I became / I'll not be,
running water's burning catharsis.

Dust
(Por)

There's nothing I hate more than dust
in corners of the room, in understanding.
But I can no longer clean everything.
I've strength enough for work, but not for cleanness.

I live in half-light. Literally half-light.
My eyes no longer tolerate the sun.
My heart can't manage all your empathies.
I don't look into death's eyes unafraid.

Because there are no gates of death, just slow
gatherings of dust. Mud and dirt cover our lives.
They gather in the corners of our souls.
We can't step into the light for fear of drowning.

Into the spider's web . . .
(A pókhálóba . . .)

God entangled in the spider's web
becomes immobile, a dummy,
woven into easily-broken
glittering threads of thought.

His trembling wings drop off, those lights,
those phosphorescences that reflect each other.
He sinks into the darkness of our twilight,
into the harbours of despair.

For just one minute liberate yourself,
erupt from our minds if only for a moment.
Let it be you that leads us through the gates
of death to the unknown far side of being.

The Translator
(A fordító)

He steps into the poem. Rock. It closes
behind him, he too becomes rock.
He becomes absorbed in the cell
of the bones, in their vaulted arcades.

But while he freezes, the clay about him
roasts at white heat, eventually melts,
and from the glowing magma there blossoms
a whole new framework, the rose in the desert.

And as for him, he turns from rock, is enclosed
within the rock, is resurrected, vanishes
on the road that leads through his body
from fullness into wholeness.

From 'Fifteen Haiku'
(A Tizenöt haiku-ból)

3.
Hot tear glows and rolls
down the desert of the face.
Earth in ice-cold space

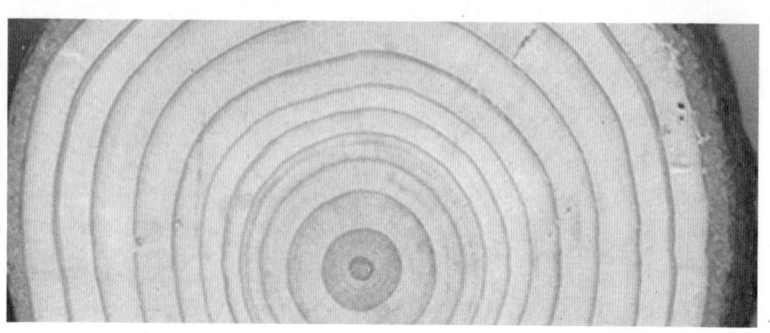

Cesare Pavese
Three poems from *Lavorare Stanca*
Translated into Scots by David Douglas

A note on the poems and the translations

In his diary (*the Business of Living*) Pavese tells us just how much work, over a period of two years, went into creating *Lavorare Stanca* (Hard Wark). Exiled to the village of Brancaleone – '*between the paws of the lion*' – following a period in prison for anti-fascist activities, Pavese observed and recreated in these 'short stories' the rhythms and landscapes of a peasant life that was in rapid transition; the younger folk swapping the harsh life of the countryside for the hard labour of the northern industrial cities and beyond.

Pavese's technique is formidable yet unobtrusive. He allows each poem to run down in just the right succession of images to a natural full stop. There is very little use of Italian's natural propensity to rhyme and, while conversational and intensely personal, very little in any of the poems that is direct dialogue.

'Maternity' is one of the most powerful poems of the collection with its recollections of a dead wife evoked in her husband's memory through the resemblance of his sons. As in all Pavese's work, there are many deft touches: life is a 'risky kind of joke' and who has not experienced that 'bewildered look' on the face of a sick relative or friend? It is a powerful reminder that for peasant women hard 'labour' is a double burden. The ending is coarser than Pavese's, but seemed to better fit the arrogance of young men out for pleasure with little regard to the consequences.

'Memories breath' expresses the exile's pleasure in those small things that in everyday life we take for granted. Towards the end of the piece, there's a hint that the return may be from political imprisonment. 'A Useless Pattern' more closely perhaps mirrors Pavese's direct experience, as a friendless, solitary, exile with few prospects.

There are many degrees of translation from the literal to the free adaptation. In transmitting the 'knot of energy' that is the pattern of an individual poem you have to accommodate the lines to this essence. Somehow the recreation must breathe with the measure and idiom of the new soundscape.

There are some poems you admire for their craft and what they create inside your head. These poems I love. The stories told could be my grandparents talking or the *auld fellas* I farmed with as a boy. I hope the man himself would have approved these recreations.

Maternity

(owre-set frae Pavese's 'Motherhood', 1998)

Three sons this man has : a big boned
body self-sufficient: watching him pass
you'd think his sons must be similar built
three young men sembling him could have sprung
unbidden frae their faithers arms
without a woman. But even wi three bodies
there's nae thing missing frae
the faithers limbs, the boys just unhooked themselves
and walkit alang aside him.

                        The woman was real enough
Had a strong body, gave her blood to her brood and died
                                            from the third.
Strange for three young lads livin without a woman
they didnae ken, who gave all her being just fer them
eclipsed hersel within them. Then the woman was young
liked to laugh and talk but taking part in life
is a risky joke. That's how she went intae silence
starin bewildered at her man.

The three sons shrug their shoulders
in a way the man remembers. None
guess or ken that their eyes and body have a life
that in its time was brim full and satisfied the man.
But watchin one o the boys as he leans
and dives intae the river, the man nae langer feels
the flash of her limbs as the body hits the watter
and then the joy of their submerged bodies. He no longer
face to face lingers if he sees his sons in the street
How lang syne his sons were born? Whae kens,
three young men arrogant now
one o them has already put one
up the spout without even baggin the woman.

Memories breath
(*owre-set frae Pavese's 'Landscape 6', 1998*)

Mist from the river rises early
wrappin the bonny town atween fields and hills
wi the smoor o memories passing. The har gathers
a the greens intae one yet women in bricht colours
walk alang. Intae the half-licht they go
smilin: here in the street anything can happen
The air wud mak ye stoatin.

                     Mornin
lays open a braid silence
that stills every voice. Even the tramp
wi nae town or hoose tae call his own will inhale it
as he breathes grappa in a glass when he's still to eat.
Its worth bein hungry or by a sweet taste
your mooth betrayed even when out an about in
                              weather like this
and findin happier memories tae breathe.
Each street, each neuk showin
In the mist an odd shudder:
feelings like this take hold. He can't give up
his calm ecstatic feel, from things
of a richer life, fresh discovered
in house or howff or from sudden thocht
Even the Clydesdales clumpin past
through the mist at dawn speak of that time.

For the boy who ran from home
and to town just today returned when the mist
from the river uncovered the town will forget the life past
of suffering, hunger and faith betrayed
as he dawdles at a corner drinkin in the mornin.
Its worth all this even if he's the only one has changed.

a useless pattern
(*adapted from Pavese's 'the morning star'*)

The man wha bides alane gets up in the morning tae licht anither fire
— a greenish star surprised bi the dawn hings nackered in the sky,
thirs naething mair bitter than a day when nocht will happen,
the slowness o time is unrelentin for a body whae expects nuthin.
The morn a lukewarm dawn and the mirk will return,
the day like yesterday naething much happened,
thirs naething mair bitter than a useless pattern,
days which streich tae nichts at the too slow tic
                     o some ancient rin-doon clock;
when the last star fades frae the sky
the man slowly pokes his fire and lichts his solitary day-ault fag.

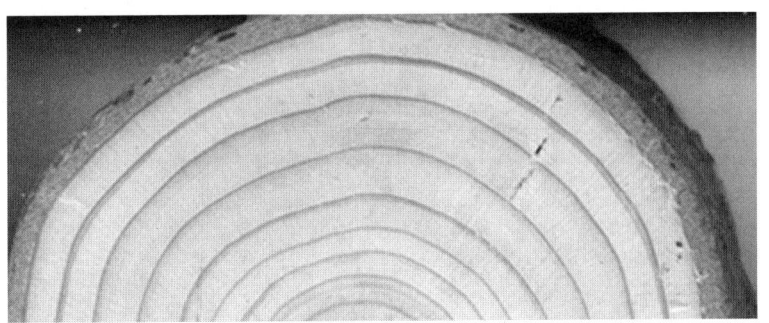

Eugeniusz Tkaczyszyn-Dycki
Five poems
Translated by Bill Johnston

The poetry of Eugeniusz Tkaczyszyn-Dycki (b. 1962) raises new questions about what a poem is, and how a poet's life relates to what he writes. Dycki (*Dits*-kee), as he is known, fills his poems with shards and shrapnel from his own life. His verse seems to be about everything and nothing at the same time. Each individual poem contains echoes of every other poem he's written, and of fragments from his own life; yet at the same time each one manages in some impalpable way to be an organic whole. Dycki's poetry is saturated with death, sickness, ambivalent and ambiguous sexuality, and a permanent identity crisis (though he chose Polish as his literary language, Dycki is from the remote southeastern part of Poland and his family is both Polish and Ukrainian). Above all, one has the sense that through all of Dycki's nine books of poetry to date, he is in a significant sense writing and re-writing one and the same poem. In a phrase from another poem of his, he has chosen 'poetry as a place on earth', yet it is a vast place in which he is constantly in motion.

Peregrinary, the first book-length selection of Dycki's poems to appear in English, will be published by Zephyr Press in Fall 2008 in Bill Johnston's translations.

my friend is sick . . .

my friend is sick
and has wrapped himself like an infant in the pain of birth
his body in which there is hope for my body
is now on the way like an apple branch in blossom

he gives a sign and like a fructifying branch means nothing
my friend is ill and his body trembles
my friend is dying and I bring him exhaustion
a sleep unrefuted by any breath

before I discovered your death . . .

before I discovered your death in the room
on the eleventh floor and saw it in the astonishment
of your nakedness and before I discovered death as a thing
that comes after breakfast lunch and dinner

I realized that the one who lay before me
in last night's bedding and the one lying in lilies
was my friend was my physiology was above all
my friend and my physiology

a thing that is holy

the women I spent nights with . . .

the women I spent nights with did not hide the fact
that they spent nights with me and they were not ashamed
when the dawn found us naked on both sides of time
the women desired to hold back that time

and remember past time as they would a child
who fell from their loins and died at once
the men I spent nights with did not hide the fact
that they spent the night alongside this child

schizophrenia is a house . . .

1.
schizophrenia is a house
of God since I fell ill
a second time and awoke
in a fever of love

truly unbelief is like a fetter
and a flaming band
in which I was ashamed of myself
though it is no shame to engage

with being and I did not squander
the light of the soul I exclaimed Lord
unbelief is the miraculous place
that I abandon daily for someone else

2.
schizophrenia is a house
of God since I fell ill
a second time and awoke
in a fever of love

Lord I exclaimed behold I am
ready to cherish things
intimate and boundless
like a dog I have restored myself

to Thee to things intimate
and boundless which I never
had and that must be why
I have been detained here so long

Song for Funia Bełska

yesterday I died
and although no one shook my hand
on the far side of the river I met
the silent and singing brothers

though not one of them came up to me
nor spoke on the threshold of a house still
unseen yet already three-dimensional like any
out-of-the-way house that endures by being whitewashed

and showing white from far off yesterday
I died my body died and sin
flowed out of me like pus through my
mouth when I stood for a kiss

Jerzy Harasymowicz
Four poems
Translated by Maria Rewakowicz, with images by Swava Harasymowicz

There Was No Snow

There was no winter
in the city
but in the mountains
the snow
like a dog
sniffs your blue footsteps for me
and I chase you like a hind
you run and I don't know
if those are swirls of clouds
or your hair

Then you pause
like a graceful doe
entangled in spruce branches
of desire
Your breasts
are heavy with spring

But you know
and I know
that I can touch you only
with a poem

Wiersze miłosne, 1979 (Love Poems)

Two Glasses

They came
talked about something

Then
she combed her golden hair
like an archangel's wing

They went out .

Only two glasses
remained

With some
red love
on the bottom

Wiersze milosne, 1979 (Love Poems)

Early Spring

He opened her blouse
and beheld spring mountains

How is it possible he wondered
that the snow is still stretching
its white paws outside

Starlings whistle
in her hair

A sin takes root . . .

Erotyki, 1992 (Erotic Poems)

Bad Weather

A wind
shakes our ancestors
out of the closet

In a downpour
a horse steams like a mountain

A rowan bush
the flame-thrower
out of poetic mercy
spills flames
over the roof

Children
carry thunder
red as a lobster
in tongs

Zielnik, 1973 (Herbarium)

(For more poems by Jerzy Harasymowicz and a note on his work by Swava Harasymowicz and Seymour Mayne see *MPT* 3/9.)

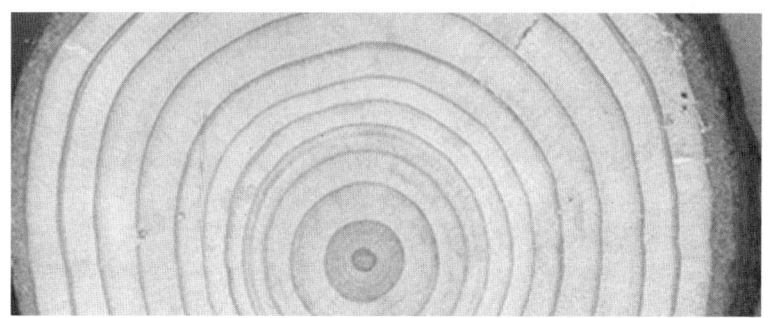

Eugene Dubnov
Two poems
Translated with the author by Vernon Scannell, Anne Ridler and John Heath-Stubbs

---

Eugene Dubnov was born in Tallinn (Estonia) in 1949; he left USSR in 1971. He was educated at Moscow, Bar-Ilan and London Universities (Psychology and English Literature). He has taught Russian, English, American and Comparative Literature. He was writer-in-residence at Carmel College, Oxfordshire (1985-87) and Wingate Scholar in London (1990-92). He has published three collections of verse in Russian and has had poems and short stories (in English translation and written in English) published in many periodicals world-wide. Nine of his short stories were broadcast on BBC Radio 3. His work has been translated into English, French, Spanish, Hebrew and German.

From 'The Flute'

       *   *   *

Not death inside the frozen slave camp
Nor execution in a blood-drenched cellar,
Not flash of axe or shattered lamp,
The poplar's cry, earth drained of colour:
Over the bitter land angry winds arise,
The storm has come to wash away the dross,
Slaking thirst, cleansing eyes
And brightening every face.

       *   *   *

Neither death nor the sea but the hoarse
And caressing voice of the flute
Moving mankind to confute
The wound at the century's source;

So summer, her arms filled with corn,
Would follow the spring, and the year
Would banish suspicion and fear,
With its seasons properly worn.

As fresh as the colour and scent
Of the lilac, the sound of the flute
Makes audible all that was mute;
From earth's confines it makes its ascent

To the great arching firmament's height:
So flautist, play on and enhance
Our life with the grace of the dance,
Of terrestrial music and light.

(London 1990–1991, translated from Russian, with the author, by Vernon Scannell)

The teachers' staffroom opened up . . .

The teachers' staffroom opened up
more or less on the river Thames;
in the Great Hall at close-packed desks
the upper sixth sat their exams.

There I was standing at a table,
watching the meadow and the bank;
impudently young, Spring entered
and made me gasp like someone drunk.

breathtaking so much beauty was;
she went on and on calling
for me to follow the stream and go
to a place with no returning.

(Translated from Russian, with the author, by Anne Ridler and John Heath-Stubbs)

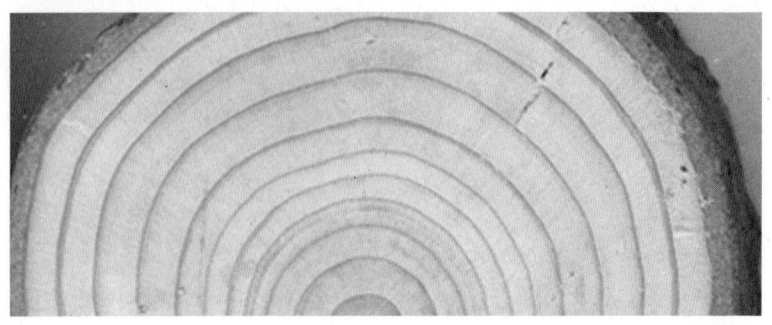

Reviews

Pura López-Colomé
Aurora
translated by Jason Stumpf
Shearsman Books
128 pp, paperback
ISBN: 978-1-905700-38-7

Dulce María Loynaz
Against Heaven, Selected Poems: a Dual Language Edition
translated by James O'Connor with a foreword by
 Juan Ramón Jiménez
Carcanet
218 pp, paperback, £14.95
ISBN: 978-1-85754-831-0

Mercedes Roffé
Like the Rains Come: Selected Poems (1987–2006)
translated by Janet Greenberg
Shearsman Books
84 pp, paperback
ISBN: 978-1-905700-55-4

Translating poetry originally written in Spanish into English can be difficult given the former's tendency to abstraction. Although these three poets very often foreground their poetic thought in imagery, one can still sense a certain tension developing between what can be termed Spanish and English poetics, made more evident in the case of the bilingual editions where there is an open invitation to read the poems alongside each other.

Such is the case with Pura López-Colomé's volume, *Aurora*. Born in Mexico City in 1952, López-Colomé is the author of nine collections of poetry, as well as a translator of poets such as Seamus Heaney, Louise Glück, and Gertrude Stein. Her own poems are lyrical, intimate and linger in the mind of the reader, like the first rays of the sun at dawn, allowing to 'thread together' what is otherwise 'hardly visible', thus calling to mind the central metaphor of the volume's title. The collection is divided into five sections each of which seems to inhabit a magical space between worlds, between light and darkness, dream and reality, nature and the human world. Sequences of poems abound, allowing for this journey through space and time, seasons and ages to develop: 'A buen resguardo' ('To Good Shelter') opens with 'the other world' moving on to 'this world' where a man builds the roof of his house, producing sound with no echo, yet searching for the *aurora* as he toils. Untitled poems are also common, drawing our attention to writing as an ongoing process, closely linked to the cycles of nature, of day and night. So she says in the poem that opens the section 'Night':

Day had shone
its finest robes.
Vanishing,
the outline of its seduction
left a wall of penetrating
scent:
night sky of magnificent
clarity.

These lines create poems that capture the lyricism and insight of the original. At other times, the translations reveal slight misreadings of the Spanish text, where *compartirse* in Spanish (meaning 'to share') becomes 'to partake' in English or *'Plegaria'* (a sort of prayer) becomes 'Pledge'. Translating is always about choices, informed by many factors, but it becomes more difficult to account for certain choices where the English poem seems to be saying something entirely different from the Spanish original. In the Translator's Acknowledgements Jason Stumpf thanks Pura López-Colomé 'for her guidance and encouragement along the way'. One wonders about the nature of this contact between translator and writer. When a poet knows the target language well and is herself a translator, one could think of the translation as a process of negotiation, an opportunity for the exploration of both languages and their respective *poetics*. In this case, though, there are some missed opportunities, given the fact that Pura López-Colomé is a poet who weighs words carefully, sensually, who is at all times aware of the conjuring power of words, their 'living, mysterious / weight'.

Something entirely different happens with James O'Connor's translations of the poetry of Dulce María Loynaz. In the first place, *Against Heaven* is a very different kind of volume: it is a scholarly edition, without being overwhelming, complete with a foreword by Juan Ramón Jiménez, and an Introduction, Chronology and list of Further Reading. O'Connor does an exhaustive job in providing the reader with the necessary background to understand the full significance of the life and work of this incredible Cuban poet. 'Man is a stupendous antagonism', reads the epigraph to the Introduction, thus summing up her work in one short line. Born in 1902, she was nearly ninety when she was awarded the Cervantes Prize from the *Real Academia Española*. Having lived through the Revolution of 1959, she was among the artists who opted to stay in Cuba, and thus suffered the humiliation and censorship of the Castro regime, while at the same time she was shunned by the exiled writers who saw her decision as a betrayal to Cuba. Her choice also brought silence and solitude and even the separation from her husband for twelve years. Yet, as O'Connor explains, solitude, love (in absence) had always been major themes in her work: 'This dichotomy of presence-in-absence, or love born of solitude, is the defining theme of Loynaz's poetry.'

The poems, selected from various volumes, from *Versos 1920–1938*, to *Últimos días de una casa* (1958) and, following a thirty-year silent gap, *La novia de Lázaro* (1991) and *Melancolía de otoño*, published posthumously in 1997, offer the first comprehensive selection and translation of Loynaz's poetry in beautifully-rendered English. O'Connor succeeds in capturing what is particular about Loynaz's voice and of finding ways of writing it as English poetry, not always an easy task, given the fact that Loynaz's poetry is often overtly religious and unafraid of expressing emotions directly:

My sorrow is as serene as moonlight.
Like the tremulous green of water
or of a breeze through the trees.
Like a shimmering breeze.
        (from 'Mi tristeza es suave' / 'My Serene Sorrow')

The 'Poems with no Names' are further examples of Loynaz's distinct voice: direct, brave, concerned with love, and its absence, as well as death and religion, though her poems are always rooted in the earth, not 'heaven', as O'Connor explains. Philosophical and almost aphoristic in nature, these poems move towards prose in a subtle, rhythmic way: 'In every grain of sand there is a landslide,' she says in 'Poem XXIX,' or 'You poured through my heart like the light that streams though the fisherman's loaded net' ('Poem LXV'), both examples of poet and translator skilfully compressing poetic thought into a handful of words.

In reading these pages one discovers a life devoted to writing. Worth highlighting is the moving poignancy of 'The Bride of Lazarus' (1991), as well as the sense of closure in 'Autumn Melancholy' (1997), which one cannot but read biographically, though these poems were probably written in the 1920s, as is the case of this one-line poem: 'This cruel stubborn silence is the sin of pride I commit against heaven and earth' ('Poem

XXXIII'). There are also occasions where the poems in English are a few lines longer than the Spanish originals. One can account for additions by looking at the constraints of grammar or the way the metaphors work in Spanish and resist the English; on other occasions, rhythm and internal rhymes seem to guide the translator: 'There are people in this world who would if they could rip a ray of light down from the moon to tie a knot in one of their boots' ('Poem XXI'), while the Spanish reads: '*Hay gente que si pudiera, arrancaría los rayos de luna, para amarrarse los zapatos*'. In any case, this volume reads as the work of a poet paying a much deserved tribute to another poet, a translator / poet who is sympathetic to the inner vision of the poems and thus truer to the spirit than to the literalness of the words.

Like Loynaz's, Mercedes Roffé's *Like the Rains Come* is also the first book-length volume to be published in English translation, though, unlike the Loynaz, it is not a bilingual edition. Roffé has been widely published in Latin America and Spain and translated into various languages. She currently divides her time between Buenos Aires and New York, where she has founded Pen Press, Plaquettes de Poesía, a small press devoted to the publication of Spanish-language poets as well poets in Spanish translation. The poems in this selection come from four collections, spanning almost two decades, from *The Lower Chamber* (1987) to *Mayan Definitions* (2006). Concerned primarily with time, with what time does to people and places, these poems deal with myth and history, with names and cultures, where the personal cannot but turn political, yet remain always lyrical, magical. 'As it is said of a transmission – deferred' ('Poem XXVII'), these poems enter the reader's consciousness gradually, like water seeping through layers of stone, they offer revelations, if not images, reflections on what we say or do not say ('the inanity of saying / just words') and succeed in creating myths out of their own world: 'the poem as myth – in the sense of synthesis and of conglomeration of meaning; as shortcut for thinking and feeling, in all its shrillness, a fragment, the intersection of any two axes of a given reality which, otherwise, would fade in the minutiae of its own obscenity' ('Poem XXXVII'). And this is precisely the logic of poetry: that everything is possible / impossible, that meaning is like water: 'the drop pierces the stone and the stone the puddle' so words merge organically to reveal the flux and continuous making and unmaking of poetic thought.

Perhaps the fact this is an English-only edition allows for a reading of these poems as 'English' (or, rather, American); the rhythm and cadence of some of the poems (the 'Three Preludes', for example), as well as their layout, would also justify this. Yet there are numerous instances where you can imagine the translator carefully weighing the words, intent on achieving a fine balance between the foreignness of the poetic vision and diction, with their tendency towards abstraction, and the constraints of what works well as poetry in the English language.

Cecilia Rossi

Richard Burns
The Blue Butterfly
Salt
148pp, paperback, £11.95
ISBN 1-844712-58-3

Richard Burns's *The Blue Butterfly* is one of the many volumes in his ongoing set of *Selected Writings*, testament to the renewed attention now enjoyed by – in the words of George Szirtes – 'one of the major half-hidden poets of England', as well as to the long route the composition has taken: this definitive form of *The Blue Butterfly* is a coming together of material amassed in the course of twenty years. In the meantime, several poems have already been housed in journals or previous collections, fragments of a whole whose structures and lines grew organically, gradually reaching a synchrony of elements and vision. Together with *The*

Manager, the long 'verse-paragraph' poem published in 2001 after a similarly protracted gestation, a certain 'blue butterfly' has been the other major creative topos of Burns, even though inhabited through sporadic glimpses and distilled segments. Yet it is indicative of the quality and anticipation surrounding the 'work-in-progress' that an early, unpublished draft was the recipient of the Wingate-Jewish Quarterly Award for Poetry as early as 1991.

Already epic in scope, the book promises to be part of an even larger synthesis, a projected 'Balkan Trilogy'. The second part, *In a Time of Drought*, a book-length sequence inspired by pan-Balkan rain ceremonies, was also published in 2006. Then, late 2008 will see the publication of *Under Balkan Light*, a collection of poems arising from Burns's intimate engagement with the peoples and cultures of the region. The poet in the midst of this publishing commotion – a companion volume offering perspectives on his work is also forthcoming – does not belong to a 'group' or 'school' and attempts at categorization are further frustrated by the fact that Burns seems at home in any form: from *poesia visiva* and evocative vignettes to long, metrically elaborate constructions. What distinguishes his work is its frequent immersion in meeting points of history and experience, in cultural otherness, in a differing consciousness that is often grounded in an alien zone – for example, Italy, Greece, Serbia – which implies an act of translation if it is to be read adequately by an anglophone reader. In *The Blue Butterfly*, this propensity finds an apposite theme in a massacre of Serbs at Kragujevac in October 1941, during the Nazi occupation of Yugoslavia. The book is an elegy, but, paradoxically, among the mourners are not only the voices of imagined survivors but also those of the dead themselves, whom the poet hears, or imagines he overhears. Part of the task the poet sets himself is to enable these voices to live again in poetry, so that we may inhabit what should not be forgotten.

The origins of a poetry that assumes such a task are themselves of interest: the book's frontispiece is a photograph of the blue butterfly, landing on Burns's 'writing hand' in May 1985 outside the 21 October Memorial Museum in Šumarice. The first stanzas began to emerge soon afterwards. Furthermore, this is a 'Jew's hand, born out of ghettos and shtetls, / raised from unmarked graves of my obliterated people / in Germany, Latvia, Lithuania, Poland, Russia'. So the story of the particular hand upon which the butterfly has come to rest itself coincides with a panorama of genocide. The period of twenty-one years that intervened between the 'calling' of the poet to this work and the finished book indicates not only the power and durability of that talismanic incident on the creative intellect but also the sheer depths of time that need to be plummeted if translation into literary expression is to be achieved at all. Early on in the first section of the book, there is a three-part poem entitled 'The Telling', each part glossed as an 'attempt'. Written deep into the fabric of this endeavour is a multiple awareness – of limits to be transcended, of a responsibility to be undertaken, of tragedy reaching out for adequate language, and of the words that finally have been chosen, struggling for justice:

> . . . Ah, but plausible
> though it may be to trust most of the time
> in language, in telling, in the passable
> undistorted transparencies of the word,
> how shall miracle, resistant, absurd,
> ring clean through the slickened varnish of rhyme?
> ('The Telling: third attempt')

What follows is a constant finding of ways. From the two German Command documents that become 'found poems' – their pragmatic cruelty only intensified as they break into lines – to the anger and sorrow captured in 'The Death of Children' and subsequent 'dialogue-poems' between 'a mother' and 'a father'; and from the lengthy, meditative sequences that make up 'Flight of the Imago' to the two lines of 'War Again: Yugoslavia 1991', Burns employs a plethora of viewpoints and expressive means in the service of a greater telling of loss. The book's classical structure of seven sections, each consisting of seven poems, reveals an alternation of modes: seven wreaths, seven 'songs' of the dead, seven statements of survivors, and seven 'blessings', that are only granted in the book's final section. Through and across these phases, the sequence charts a psychological progression from impossible suffering to desired redemption. The variety of rhyme schemes combines with the integrative agility of the composition to register many voices: among them, the last words of the dying, in fragments of letters that speak across time; intertextualised readings of the I Ching; and translations of two songs from the cycle *Mauthausen* by the Greek poet Iakovos Kampanellis, who was himself deported to that concentration camp.

The inclusion of such varied material itself suggests completeness of experience within a work of empathy and commemoration. The text of the poem is followed by photographic records of the massacre, coupled with heart-rending 'last messages', leading into a postscript that reflects on the inception and development of the poems and offers copious notes on the terrible events at Kragujevac from Burns's research. Alongside the poetic composition, these are a vital part of this work, mirroring the force of the real and evidencing a living poetry that meshes literature and experienced history, one potently articulating the other.

Despite the focus on a single event, *The Blue Butterfly* at several points hints at understandings of a wider 'natural history of destruction' – to borrow the poignant English title of W. G. Sebald's book on literature and the air raids of the Second World War – as well as the very human capacity for what is named through a 'conference of tongues' in the last lines of 'Nada: Hope or Nothing': 'a blue butterfly takes my hand and writes / in invisible ink across its page of air / Nada, Elpidha, Nadezhda, Esperanza, Hoffnung'. Ultimately, this kind of stirring, multifaceted, 'embedded' poetry operates simultaneously as mediator and enabler: it confronts the unspeakable parts of ourselves and the darknesses of shared history, as it searches for spiritual strength and necessary reconciliation in times of seemingly unending violence. It is then perhaps not surprising that even before the publication of this first edition in English, much of this book has already been translated into Serbian and other Balkan languages; even while this long, composite poem was still evolving in a foreign tongue, it was being internalised by the Slav inheritors of the original wound.

Paschalis Nikolaou

Elena Shvarts
Birdsong on the Seabed
translated by Sasha Dugdale,
Bloodaxe Books
176 pp £9.95
ISBN 978-1-85224-783-6

The calibre of the St Petersburg poet Elena Shvarts (b. 1948) is such that she deserves a wide readership abroad. We can thus be grateful to Bloodaxe for providing us with a showcase of her work via two bilingual texts: *'Paradise': Selected Poems* (1993) translated by Michael Molnar (with additional translations by Catriona Kelly) and this latest collection *Birdsong on the Seabed* (2008) from Sasha Dugdale. Both translators, though different in their approach, create poetry tuned to the modern ear and, working closely with Shvarts, provide insightful introductions to the poetry. Molnar shows how Shvarts builds on St Petersburg's literary tradition as a city variously violent, heavenly, satanic or surreal, while Dugdale, whilst reinforcing Molnar's argument, goes on to analyse Shvarts as a 'poet of fevered visionary experiences', one who, though deeply religious, stands outside orthodoxy. It is not surprising to find both are Poetry Book Society Choices. Also, because Dugdale translates poems from Shvarts' numerous post-'93 collections, the texts work well as companion volumes.

Dugdale takes us through Shvarts' whole range via selections from five collections along with poems not yet published in Russia. We start off with the St Petersburg theme that dominates the whole of Molnar's selection. Violence and passion are inseparable, as in 'If you and I should think to die – ' with its startling river image suggesting both the city's bloody history and its severe weather: 'And the Neva's cut-throat razor/ Shears life's threads' counterbalanced by the affectionate concluding lines:

> Let me kiss you, ice-flown river
> Let me drop you, moon, to shatter
> In the waves.

From here the poetry provides a whirlwind journey through the cosmos, a kind of joyous pessimism at the moment of apocalypse such as in 'The Last Night':

> The constellations are gone. There is a mad snow
> From the wild dancing stars, from the flames,
> Selene suddenly snaps with a jingling,
> But Life is still living, till the morning of day.

Shvarts conveys frenzied, overstretched emotions that edge into the surreal or a dream state, shifting the boundaries between self and world, like Tolstoy's pantheism in reverse, so that rather than a harmonious merging of self and world there is a violent disintegration of a self flung to the four winds as in the following untitled poem:

> What torment living is
> On this Midsummer's night
> Better, to be a dark spirit
> And fly over fields in light.
> Better to shed all flesh
> And enter the dandelion

> And with a single breath
> Be scattered far and wide.

She is a clear descendent of Marina Tsvetaeva but with the heat turned up, seen in the way poetry transcends the laws of physics as in 'Poetica – more geometrico': 'Parallel lines intersected/ A haven's red light in the angle created', and the portrayal of the poet as pariah, but one who willingly accepts her fate such as 'When I fly over the dark waters':

> When an angel carries away my soul
> All shrouded in fog, folded in flames
> I have no body, no tears to weep
> Just a bag in my heart, full of poems.

Sasha Dugdale is the ideal translator of Shvarts on a number of counts: along with a five years' residency in Russia she is a fine poet herself (see both her Carcanet/Oxford Poets collections: *Notebook* (2003) and her more recent *The Estate* (2007)), but most importantly, in her own poems she uses both traditional forms and free verse and with translation attempts to recreate something of the rhyme and metre of the original. This is vital with Shvarts' poetry because of her unconventional techniques, as Dugdale explains in the introduction: 'Most often the impression of "taking flight" is created by deviation from metrical patterns, which destabilises those patterns without letting go of them entirely.' For the vast proportion of this collection Dugdale shows herself to be a real master of the subtle pararhyme, half rhyme and assonance mirroring Shvarts' verse. Consider the rhymes in 'The Christmas Mystery in Kolomna':

> The night-blue curtain conjures a scene:
> Bethlehem's warm winter scent –
> The breath of the ox, the dung's sweet steam
> More precious than gold or frankincense.

There is the odd glitch which tends to be when she attempts to replicate originals containing full end rhymes, as in 'If you and I should think to die – ': 'If you and I should think to die – / Why not? We'll nick a van and fly' or further in the same poem: 'Start her up and off we go, / The van dances, judders so', lines reminiscent of a Janet and John reading primer. Fortunately these are rare but they stand out dramatically because of the subtle rhyming that dominates the book.

Ultimately, though, what makes Dugdale such a rarity in the small world of Russian translation is that she manages to work with her foot in both camps: it is unusual to find a translator working within traditional forms who possesses a poet's eye such as hers, focussed on the end product to the extent that they'll risk freeing themselves from the shackles of the literal for the sake of a great line in the spirit of the original. It is the intelligent way that she mixes flexibility with formality that makes her a safe pair of hands for presenting Shvarts's startling poems to an English-speaking public.

Belinda Cooke

Haven and Prison

Jeni Williams and Latéfa Guémar (editors)
Fragments from the Dark
Hafan Books 2008

Humberto Gatica
The Sand Garden/El Jardin de Arena
Hafan Books 2008
(both can be ordered at www.hafan.org/orderform.htm)

Marc Falkoff (editor)
Poems from Guantánamo
University of Iowa Press 2007

True to their name, Hafan Books are a place of refuge. More, they are a place in which refugees of various kinds can collect themselves and say what their lives are like. Humberto Gatica is a poet and photographer who, after ten months in a brutal jail, got out of Pinochet's Chile, finally settling with his wife in Swansea. His poems face one another in two thin columns, Spanish and English, across the opening pages, black and white photographs interleaving them. Stark, exact, unsentimental. A cold wind whistles through them: breath nevertheless. *Fragments from the Dark*, on the other hand, is a crowded book, dozens of voices, some speaking their own languages – Welsh, English, French, Arabic – some translated, all women and girls, prose and poems, interviews, fragments. Also there are pictures, by two little sisters, for example, who look after their mother and their younger sister. Picture of a house 'The place where I would like to live', picture of the ailing mother. The total suffering here is great. But the refuge, this book, certainly a very haunted place, contradicts by its variety, energy and solidarity the misfortune and injustice that collectively it remembers and makes known. If Brecht's three gods still trail the earth looking for reasons why they should not obliterate humankind, they will surely spare us a while longer should they light on Swansea Bay Asylum Seekers Support Group and the fortifying sanctuary of Hafan Books.

And we might get a further reprieve if the same exhausted trio ever come across *Poems from Guantánamo* and meet Marc Falkoff, Ariel Dorfman, Flagg Miller or any of the mostly unnamed translators of these poems out of an infamous jail. Contemplating Guantánamo we do badly need reasons not to despair. For there is something quite peculiarly dispiriting in the public spectacle of a nation, a legal entity, a subscriber to the rule of law, acting unjustly. A nation powerful enough to act as it chooses, and choosing to act unjustly. And hearing the injustice defended, or redefined so as not to be an injustice after all, and witnessing it being connived at and tactfully looked away from, how shaming that is. Those elected spokespersons being themselves quite shameless, somehow it shames us, the electorate, even to watch and hear them. The enduring wrong of it, the risible hypocrisy of their still uttering the word 'freedom'. Wrong and stupid. Very very stupid. Poems, which the prisoners understand as a way of asserting their humanity, are viewed by the Pentagon as 'a special risk' to national security, because of their 'content and format'; which, being interpreted, means that the Pentagon — whose phrase for the prisoners' suicide attempts is 'manipulative self-injurious behaviour' — fear truthful speech, as something deeply foreign. Moazzam Begg, a British citizen detained in Guantánamo for three years without charge, had a letter in there from his seven-year old daughter so censored that only one line of it — 'I love you, Dad' — was legible. When he got out she told him that the obliterated lines were 'One, two, three, four, five,/ Once I caught a fish alive./ Six, seven, eight, nine, ten,/ Then I let it go again.' This intelligent book, with its poems, harrowing brief biographies and editorial essays, is an act of opposition. It is raised up by the prisoners themselves, by the volunteer lawyers working on their behalf, by the translators who could not consult the poets they were translating, by the essayists and by Iowa University Press to oppose a wrongdoing. Law in action against injustice; intelligence against stupidity; the truth of poetry against mendacity; translation through barbed wire.

David Constantine

Further Books I: Recycling the past

Paul Batchelor, *The Sinking Road*, Bloodaxe Books, paperback, 64pp, £7.95, ISBN: 978-1-85224807-9

Maureen Almond & Glyn Goodrick, *Recollections*, Flambard Press, paperback, 60pp, £10, ISBN: 978-1-873226-97-1

Jane Holland, *Lament of the Wanderer*, Heaventree, paperback, 21pp, £4, ISBN: 978-1-906038-06-9

John Lucas, I ,*The Poet Egil: Versions of the poems of Egil's Saga*, Redbeck Press, paperback, 45pp, £8, ISBN: 978-1-904338-40-6

George Chapman, *Homeric Hymns & Other Homerica*, Edited by Allardyce Nicoll, Introduced by Stephen Scully, Princeton University Press, paperback, £9.95, ISBN: 978-0-691-13676-9

From Fitzgerald's transgressions of the *Rubaiyat* through Pope's version of the *Iliad* – the 'pretty poem' which may or may not be Homer – to the more recent engagements of Seamus Heaney's *Beowulf* or Ted Hughes' *Tales from Ovid*, the translation of classic texts and the writing of original poetry have long been mutually intertwined. Certainly the relationship between classical translation and creative writing is usually a happy one, benefiting both translator/writer and original text in the new understandings and insights such work often brings to both source and target text.

It is therefore satisfying to see new generations of poets continuing this tradition. *The Sinking Road*, Paul Batchelor's first collection for Bloodaxe, references the classical world in his free versions of Ovid's *Tristia* or classical myth in 'Artemis' and 'Pygmalion's Prayer to Venus'. Elsewhere he mines ancient Celtic saga, such as the Welsh *Mabinogion* for 'Blodeuwedd', or the 9th century Irish cycle of 'Suibne Changed', while 'Gilgamesh Rebukes Istah' (like Batchelor's *Tristia*, first published in *MPT*), turns to the Sumerian epic of Gilgamesh, one of literature's earliest surviving poems. Meanwhile more recent history, both personal and cultural, sits alongside a plethora of other influences ranging from the high culture of Robin Fulton's translations of Tomas Tranströmer to the hip culture of an album by late 70s band Magazine. Batchelor's diverse points of reference are held in place by a web of natural imagery throughout – yew, hawthorn, the lingering scent of household plants – delicate and precious echoes of the past 'easily carried/ easily held/ between finger & thumb/ as if for safe keeping'.

Poet Maureen Almond and photographer Glyn Goodrick's collection *Recollections* also excavates antiquity to give voices – and images – to long-lost echoes of a forgotten past. The collection, commissioned by the Museum of Antiquities at Newcastle University, features 28 beautifully-composed photographs of the Museum's finest Roman artefacts from Goodrick, alongside Almond's haunting and compelling poems inspired by and/ or complementing each one. A 2nd century mortarium from South Shields, photographed by Goodrick with a delicately-lit sprig of fresh herbs, sets the tone: 'Take a couple of hundred Roman soldiers,' begins Almond's facing poem, 'A Recipe for Englishness', 'spice them up with notions of Empire,/ add one Governor, sick for Rome . . .'

Goodrick's imaginative photography provides the perfect foil for Almond's skilful re-imagining of ancient artefacts (her previous collection *The Works* transposed Horace's *Epodes* to working-class Teesside) so that ancient and modern, text and image, balance in perfectly-judged equilibrium throughout; a shield boss photographed on a bed of moss and lichen ('Maybe you saw the writing on the wall,' muses Almond's 'Towards the End', 'realised that in the end, you'd lose') or a skilfully shadowed hair comb ('young men's secrets caught between the teeth,' as 'DNA' imagines). As *The Works* illustrated, Almond is justly proud of her local heritage – a heritage Goodrick's visuals are happy to reference, sometimes with tongue firmly placed in cheek; a relief of the goddess Fortuna from Newcastle, for instance, is depicted with a bottle of the city's famous Brown Ale. 'Your wings/ are still buried/ in our muddy river/ yet you offer, with your right hand,/ a drink,' notes Almond's characteristically affirming accompanying poem: 'Fortune,/ you smiled on us./ First angel of the North,/ from your horn of plenty you filled/ the Tyne.' With its multi-faceted approach to all forms of translation and excavation, both visual and verbal, this is a marvellous book. As 'A Recipe for Englishness' concludes: 'Pour into olive-oiled black-burnished bowls/ and leave to set for two thousand years.'

Like Batchelor, both Jane Holland and John Lucas also find inspiration in ancient saga. Lucas's *I, The Poet Egil* collects together some of his earlier versions of the medieval Icelandic *Egil's Saga*, first published in the Dent Everyman edition in 1975, here linking them with a new prose narrative to explain the context of each. As Lucas explains in his Introduction, finding contemporary equivalents for the compound metaphors of such works is an impossible task, nevertheless his versions, like Egil's raised sword, cut to the quick of the original: 'to stand tall in the prow,/ to steer the vessel well,/ to hold for harbour and/ hack down man after man.' By contrast, Jane Holland's pamphlet, *Lament of the Wanderer*, presents a new, feminised reading of the much-interpreted Anglo-Saxon poem, which, as she explains in a brief introductory note, 'happened quite naturally and which I did not resist'. It's a fascinating, if controversial, approach, like Almond's & Goodrick's *Recollections,* linking past and present grief to great effect, as the ever-present threat of destruction echoes to us across the centuries: 'Those things/ we most fear to lose are only lent to us:/ our coins, our companions, our loved ones, our lives./ and one day, even the earth's account/ shall stand empty.'

Last but by no means least, we come to the master of classical translation to show us all how it is done. George Chapman's 1642 versions of the so-called *Homeric Hymns*, a collection of 33 poems dedicated to the Greek Pantheon, now known to be composed by an unknown poet or poets around 650BC, are not as well known – or perhaps as well-thought of – as his translations of Homer's epic *Iliad* and *Odyssey*, immortalised in Keats' sonnet. Nevertheless, Princeton's reprint of the 1956 Bollingen Series edition is a very welcome addition to an understanding of Chapman's art. As Stephen Scully points out in his helpful introduction, Chapman's versions are of historical and literary interest to us, both as the first edition of the *Hymns* in English but also because they tell us much of the 'Renaissance effort to make Homer out of them'. Chapman's strategy, Scully notes, was to attack archaic Greek's tricky compound epithets with vigour, often adding more to his English text and underscoring them with end rhyme: 'All haile (O blest Latona!) to bring forth/ An issue of such All-out-shining worth,' as his *Hymne to Apollo* asserts.

Chapman's efforts were not always so overlooked; Shelley was so inspired by reading such 'magical verses' that he began translating the *Hymns* himself, although an eye illness forced him to abandon the project after completing just five. Today we can recognise the enormous debt owed by all subsequent classical translators to Chapman's efforts to marry Greek epic idiom to the sometimes inhospitable context of English verse: 'So I salute thee still,' as his 'To Pallas' concludes, 'and still in praise/ Thy Fame and others', shall my Memorie raise.'

Josephine Balmer

Books for review should be sent to Josephine Balmer, Reviews Editor, *Modern Poetry in Translation*, East Meon, St John's Road, Crowborough, East Sussex. UK. TN6 1RW.

Notes on Contributors

Josephine Balmer's collections include *Sappho: Poems and Fragments; Classical Women Poets; Catullus: Poems of Love and Hate* and *Chasing Catullus: Poems, Translations and Transgressions* (all Bloodaxe). She is a judge for The Times/Stephen Spender Prize for Poetry in Translation and Royal Literary Fund Writing 2007/8 Writing Fellow at the University of Sussex. *The Word for Sorrow* (much of which first appeared in *MPT*) will be published by Salt in Spring 2009.

Chris Beckett grew up in Ethiopia in the 1960s. He won the *Poetry London* competition in 2001 and his first collection, *The Dog Who Thinks He's A Fish*, was published in 2004. He is working on a collection of praise poems about boyhood in Ethiopia.

Anne Cluysenaar, born Belgium, Irish citizen, runs a smallholding in Wales. Among her publications: *Timeslips, New and Selected Poems* (Carcanet 1997); *Batu-Angas: Envisioning Nature with Alfred Russel Wallace* (Seren 2008); autobiographical poems, *Water to Breathe* (forthcoming Flarestack 2008). Featured in *Poetry 1900–2000, One hundred poets from Wales* (Parthian 2008).

Mary-Ann Constantine is a research fellow at the University of Wales. Among her publications are *Breton Ballads (1996)* and *The Truth against the World, Iolo Morganwg and Romantic Forgery* (2007). Her short stories have appeared in *Planet* and in the *New Welsh Review*.

Belinda Cooke's poetry, reviews and Russian translations have been published widely. She is currently completing an edition of *The Selected Writings of Marina Tsvetaeva*. She lives in Aberdeenshire.

Notes on Contributors

Anna Crowe's latest poetry collection is *Punk with Dulcimer* (Peterloo 2006), translated into Spanish as *Punk con salterio* (4 Estaciones 2008). She is co-founder of StAnza, Scotland's poetry festival. In 2005 she was awarded a Travelling Scholarship from the Society of Authors. Her translations of poems by the Catalan poet Joan Margarit, *Tugs in the fog* (Bloodaxe 2006) received a PBS Recommendation.

Jason Walford Davies is Senior Lecturer in the School of Welsh and Co-Director of the R.S. Thomas Study Centre at Bangor University. He has published extensively on the work of R.S. Thomas, and is currently writing a biography of Waldo Williams for University of Wales Press. In 2004 he won the Crown at the National Eisteddfod of Wales; a collection of his poems, *Rhwng Dau Olau*, will be published in 2009.

David Douglas, after years of travelling as a research mineralogist then as project manager, now writes and lives in a Galloway village not five miles from where he started. A selection of his work in Scots appears in *Chuckies fir the Cairn* (Luath, 2008). Currently he is adapting the *Foras Feasa ar Eirinn* by Sethrun Ceitinn and is completing a sequence on various facets of modernism called *Ezra's Children*.

Cindy Eisner is a computer scientist by profession. She translated her first poem, Porat's *In Netanya, On the Cliff*, in 2005.

Terry Gifford is author of *Ted Hughes* (2008), *Reconnecting With John Muir: Essays in Post-Pastoral Practice* (2006), *The Unreliable Mushrooms: New and Selected Poems* (2003), *Pastoral* (1999) and *Green Voices: Understanding Contemporary Nature Poetry* (1995; 2009). He is Visiting Professor at the University of Chichester, UK, and Profesor Honorario at the University of Alicante, Spain.

Swava Harasymowicz, artist and illustrator, Krakow-born and based in London since 1998. Winner of the Arts Foundation 2008 Fellowship in Illustration. Graduate of the Royal College of Art, studied English Philology in Krakow. Current projects include a self-generated graphic novel.

Ellen Hinsey is the author of *Update on the Descent* (forthcoming 2009), *The White Fire of Time* and *Cities of Memory*. She has edited and translated (with Constantine Rusanov) *The Junction: Selected Poems of Tomas Venclova* (Bloodaxe Books 2008). Her poems and essays have appeared in *The New York Times, The New Yorker* and *Poetry Review* and elsewhere. She has received a Berlin Prize Fellowship, a Rona Jaffe Foundation Award and a Lannan Foundation Award.

Mike Horwood was born in London in 1955 and has lived in Finland since 1985. He is studying on Manchester Metropolitan University's online M.A. in creative writing and his poems have appeared in many magazines and anthologies.

Since 1999, **Naomi Jaffa** has been Director of The Poetry Trust, an Arts Council flagship organisation for literature which runs the Aldeburgh Poetry Festival plus a year round programme of readings, learning and outreach, residential courses, prizes and publishing initiatives. Her pamphlet *The Last Hour of Sleep* was published by Five Leaves Press in 2003.

Bill Johnston has translated numerous works of poetry and prose from Polish. Among them are Witold Gombrowicz's *Bacacay* (Archipelago 2004), Magdalena Tulli's *Dreams and Stones* (Archipelago 2004), and Krzysztof Kamil Baczyński's *White Magic and Other Poems* (Green Integer 2005). His most recent poetry translation, Tadeusz Różewicz's *new poems* (Archipelago 2007), won the 2008 Found in Translation Award for the best translation from Polish. He is the director of the Polish Studies Center at Indiana University.

Notes on Contributors

Mark Leech's poem sequence, *London Water*, is published by Flarestack, and a virtual chapbook of his translations of Lorca is available online from Brindin Press (www.brindin.com). He lives in Oxford.

Anna Lewis, born in 1984, has won several awards for young writers, most recently the Robin Reeves Prize in 2008. Her poetry has appeared in journals including *Poetry Wales, New Welsh Review, The Interpreter's House* and *Mslexia*. She is currently working towards a first collection.

Paschalis Nikolaou received his Ph.D. from the University of East Anglia and is currently teaching and research fellow in literary translation at the Ionian University (Corfu). He is the co-editor of *Translating Selves: Experience and Identity between Languages and Literatures* (Continuum, 2008). Reviews, translations and poems have appeared in, among other magazines, *The London Magazine, MPT* and *The Wolf*.

J.P. Nosbaum was born in the United States but has lived in Britain for the last 15 years. He will shortly be moving to Seattle.

Peter Oram: born Cardiff 1947; worked as teacher and musician for many years but since the mid-90s has been independently active as writer, composer, publisher and translator. Publications include: *Maddocks* (novel, Gomer 1997), *The Rub* (novel, Starborn 2001), *White* (Poems, Starborn 2001), *The Page and the Fire* (translations of Russian Poetry of the 20th Century, Arc 2007). He now lives near Nürnberg in Germany.

Simon Patton works as a literary translator specializing in contemporary Chinese literature. He makes a living teaching Chinese language and translation at the University of Queensland. Since November 2002, he has co-edited the China domain of Poetry International Web with the Chinese poet Yu Jian at china.poetryinternationalweb.org.

Pascale Petit's last two collections *The Huntress* and *The Zoo Father* (Seren) were both shortlisted for the T S Eliot Prize. Her new collection *The Treekeeper's Tale* (Seren) is due in November 2008. She took part in the Yellow Mountain Poetry Festival in China and the UK in 2007–8 and is the Royal Literary Fund Fellow at Middlesex University 2007–9. Website: www.pascalepetit.co.uk

Allen Prowle was awarded the Times/Stephen Spender Prize 2007 for his translations of poems by Attilio Bertolucci. Previously, The Lincolnshire Association commissioned his translations of poems by Paul Verlaine to commemorate the centenary of the poet's residence in Stickney in 1875. A collection of his own poems, *Landmarks*, appeared in 1977.

Maria G. Rewakowicz, poet, translator and literary scholar, holds a Ph.D in Slavic Languages and Literatures from the University of Toronto. Currently she is a visiting lecturer in the Dept. of Slavic Languages and Literatures at the University of Washington in Seattle.

Oliver Reynolds is an usher at the Royal Opera House. His last book of poems was *Almost* (1999).

Cecilia Rossi, a poet and translator from Buenos Aires, has recently completed the translation of Alejandra Pizarnik's *Complete Poetry* for a Ph.D. at the University of East Anglia.

Sibyl Ruth is Rose Scooler's great-niece. She has published two collections of her own poems *Nothing Personal* (Iron Press 1995) and *I Could Become That Woman* (Five Leaves 2003). She lives in Birmingham. She is also the winner of this year's *Mslexia* poetry competition.

Notes on Contributors

Robert Saxton, born 1952, read English at Magdalen College, Oxford. He is the author of three books of poetry: *The Promise Clinic* (Enitharmon 1994), *Manganese* (Carcanet/OxfordPoets 2003) and *Local Honey* (Carcanet/OxfordPoets 2007). He lives in North London and is the editorial director of an illustrated book publishing company. Website: www.robertsaxton.co.uk

Sudeep Sen (www.sudeepsen.net) has written/translated/edited over a dozen books, including: *Postmarked India: New & Selected Poems* (HarperCollins), *Distracted Geographies*, and *Rain*. His poetry has been translated into twenty-five languages. Recent work by him appears in *New Writing 15* (Granta, 2007) & the Norton poetry anthology: *Language of a New Century* (Norton, 2008). He is the editorial director of Aark Arts, editor of *Atlas* & lives in New Delhi & London.

Jo Shapcott, born 1953, teaches on the MA in Creative Writing at Royal Holloway. She is also a Visiting Professor at Newcastle University and the London Institute and Royal Literary Fund Fellow at Oxford Brookes. *Her Book: Poems 1988-1998* is a selection of poems from individual volumes: *Electroplating the Baby* (1988), which won the Commonwealth Poetry Prize for Best First Collection, *Phrase Book* (1992), and *My Life Asleep* (1998), which won the Forward Poetry Prize.

Pauline Stainer is a freelance writer and tutor. *Crossing the Snowline*, to be published this October, will be her first new collection since *The Lady and the Hare: New and Selected Poems* (Bloodaxe 2003) which draws on five previous books, as well as a new collection, *A Litany of High Waters*. Her fourth collection *The Wound-Dresser's Dream* was shortlisted for the Whitbread Poetry Award in 1996..

George Szirtes was born in Budapest, in 1948, and came to England as a refugee in 1956. He studied art in London and Leeds. His first book, *The Slant Door* (1979), was joint winner of the Faber Memorial Prize. His twelfth, *Reel* (2004), was awarded the T S Eliot Prize. His *New and Collected Poems* appears in 2008. He has translated volumes of selected poems by Ottó Orbán, Zsuzsa Rakovszky and Ágnes Nemes Nagy, and fiction by Sándor Márai, László Krasznahorkai, Gyula Krúdy among others.

Stefan Tobler is a freelance translator from Portuguese and German. His translation of Roger Willemsen's *Afghan Journey* was a 2007 Recommended Translation from English PEN. His translations of Antônio Moura were recently awarded the BCLA Dryden translation prize's commendation and he is developing an exhibition involving the poems and would be interested to hear from possible venues (stefan.tobler@gmail.com).

Dennis Tomlinson first encountered Wulf Kirsten while writing a PhD thesis on environmental issues in East German literature. He has published several poems and reviews in small magazines, translations of Heinz Czechowski's poems in *The Wolf* magazine as well as a fantasy volume entitled *The Voice of Heaven* (2005).

Siriol Troup's poems have appeared in the *TLS, Poetry Review, PN Review, The Warwick Review, Poetry London* and other journals. Her first collection, *Drowning up the Blue End,* was published by Bluechrome in 2004. Her second collection is due from Shearsman in 2009.

MODERN POETRY IN TRANSLATION Series 3 Number 8

GETTING IT ACROSS

Edited by David and Helen Constantine

Cover by Lucy Wilkinson

Contents
Editorial   David and Helen Constantine

Bernardo Atxaga, two poems, translated by Margaret Jull Costa
Gabriela Mistral, 'The Foreigner', translated by Arthur McHugh
Niyati Keni, Poetry in Four Dimensions
Helen and David Constantine, A Language without Words
Alyss Dye, 'Word Blindness'
Moniza Alvi, 'Writing at the Centre'
Saradha Soobrayen, One Foot in England and one Foot in Mauritius
Oliver Reynolds, 'Slip'
Pascale Petit, 'I was born in the Larzac'
Annemarie Austin, 'Dysphasias'
Gregory Warren Wilson, three poems
Pedro Serrano, four poems from 'Still Life', translated by Anna Crowe
Stephanie Norgate, two haiku versions of Lucretius
Robin Fulton, four poems
Martha Kapos, two poems
Carole Satyamurti, three poems
Harry Martinson, five poems, translated by Robin Fulton
Jenny Joseph, An essay and five poems, after paintings by Jaume Prohens
Martti Hynynen, five poems, translated by Mike Horwood
Lucy Hamilton, extracts from a sonnet version of *Lalla Maghnia*
Tsvetanka Elenkova, six poems, translated by Jonathan Dunne
Tuğrul Tanyol, four poems, translated by Ruth Christie
Jane Draycott, a translation of the first two sections of *Pearl*
Naomi Jaffa, The Aldeburgh Poetry Festival
Poetry from Aldeburgh
Taha Muhammad Ali, three poems, translated by Peter Cole, Yahya Hijazi and Gabriel Levin
Michael Hamburger, four poems

Robert Walser, twelve poems, translated by Michael Hamburger
Two Memorial Notes on Michael Hamburger by Anthony Rudolf and Iain Galbraith

Reviews
Charlie Louth on Don Paterson, Martyn Crucefix and Rilke
Belinda Cooke on *The Translator as Writer* (edited by Susan Bassnett and Peter Bush)
Jo Balmer, Shorter Reviews

Price £11
  Available from www.mptmagazines.com

MODERN POETRY IN TRANSLATION   Series 3   Number 9

PALESTINE

Edited by David and Helen Constantine

Cover by Lucy Wilkinson

Contents
Instead of an Editorial
    David and Helen Constantine

Joe Sacco, from *Palestine*
Jonathan Holmes, Israel/Palestine: a Century of Violence
Mahmoud Darwish, 'Mural', translated by Rema Hammami and John Berger
Deema Shehabi, two ghazals
Marilyn Hacker, two ghazals
Jack Hamesh, two letters from Palestine to Ingeborg Bachmann, translated by David Constantine
Agi Mishol, 'Parent Poems', translated by Vivian Eden
Alan Hart, 'Volunteer 1969'
Salman Masalha, three poems translated by Vivian Eden and the author
John Berger, Concerning Identity
Dvora Amir, three poems, translated by Jennie Freldman
Jennie Feldman, 'Sage Tea'
Ghassan Zaqtan, 'Alone and the river before me', translated by Fady Joudah
Tal Nitzan, three poems, translated by Vivian Eden and the author
Vivian Eden, From Arabic to Hebrew and Hebrew to Arabic: Poetry Translation as a Microcosm of How the World Ought to Work
Yosef Sharon, 'The Shelter', translated by Gabriel Levin
Mahmoud Darwish, 'Like a Hand Tattoo' translated by Fady Joudah
Rivka Miriam, four poems translated by Linda Zisquit
Samih al-Qasim, four poems, translated by Nazih Kassis
Welcome to Bethlehem
Josephine Balmer, *The Word for Sorrow*
Bertil Malmberg, five poems, translated by Bill Coyle
Carlos Marzal, four poems, translated by Nathaniel Perry

Eeva-Liisa Manner, three poems, translated by Emily Jeremiah
Kristiina Ehin, six poems, translated by Ilmar Lehtpere
Dannie Abse, 'Dafydd ap Gwilym at Llanbadarn'
Jerzy Harasymowicz, three poems, translated by Maria Rewakowicz

Reviews
Belinda Cooke on Ted Hughes's translations
Jo Balmer, Shorter Reviews

Price £11
　Available from www.mptmagazine.com

MPT Subscription Form

Name	Address
Phone	Postcode
E-mail	Country

I would like to subscribe to *Modern Poetry in Translation* (please tick relevant box):

Subscription Rates (including postage by surface mail)

	UK	**Overseas**
❏ One year subscription (2 issues)	£22	£26 / US$ 52
❏ Two year subscription (4 issues) with discount	£40	£48 / US$ 96

Student Discount*
❏ One year subscription (2 issues)	£16	£20 / US$ 40
❏ Two year subscription (4 issues)	£28	£36 / US$ 72

Please indicate which year you expect to complete your studies 20 . . .

Standing Order Discount (only available to UK subscribers)
❏ Annual subscription (2 issues)   £20
❏ Student rate for annual subscription (2 issues)*   £14

Payment Method (please tick appropriate box)

❏ **Cheque:** please make cheques payable to: *Modern Poetry in Translation*. Sterling, US Dollar and Euro cheques accepted.

❏ **Standing Order:** please complete the standing order request below, indicating the date you would like your first payment to be taken. This should be at least one month after you return this form. We will set this up directly with your bank. Subsequent annual payments will be taken on the same date each year. For UK only.

Bank Name	Account Name
Branch Address	❏ Please notify my bank
	Please take my first payment on
Post Code	……../……../……… and future payments on
Sort Code	the same date each year.
Account Number	Signature:
	Date………/………/…………

Bank Use Only: In favour of Modern Poetry in Translation, Lloyds TSB, 1 High St, Carfax, Oxford, OX1 4AA, UK a/c 03115155 Sort-code 30-96-35

Please return this form to: The Administrator, Modern Poetry in Translation, The Queen's College, Oxford, OX1 4AW   administrator@mptmagazine/www.mptmagazine.com